ODDitude

ODDitude

Finding the Passion for Who You Are and What You Do

John R. Powers, Ph.D.

Health Communications, Inc.
Deerfield Beach, Florida

www.bcibooks.com

Library of Congress Cataloging-in-Publication Data

Powers, John R.

Odditude : finding the passion for who you are and what you do. / John Powers.

p. cm.

ISBN-13: 978-0-7573-0575-7 (trade paper)

ISBN-10: 0-7573-0575-X (trade paper)

1. Self-actualization (Psychology) 2. Eccentrics and eccentricities.

3. Success—Psychological aspects. I. Title.

BF637.S4P684 2007

158.1—dc22

2006103120

Publisher: Health Communications, Inc.
3201 S.W. 15th Street
Deerfield Beach, FL 33442–8190

Interior book design and formatting by Lawna Patterson Oldfield

To JaNelle, my loving wife,
and Jacey and Joy, my daughters.
The three corners of my world.

Contents

Acknowledgments

I would like to thank Dr. Kenneth Sorrick, the best business partner that anyone could have. Joe Durepos, who introduced me to Peter Rubie, my agent. Peter Rubie, whose talent and faith have made this book a reality. Michele Matrisciani and her staff at HCI whose work on my behalf has made this book possible. Noreen Heron and her people who have made this book an even bigger success.

Mom Was Right . . .

You are special. Well, you started out that way. We all did. Of the approximately 400 million sperm who began the journey, the only survivor was the one who played a major role in creating you. To put it another way, if your creation had been a lottery and you combined the populations of the United States, Canada, and Mexico, you would have been the only winner.

Each of us began life as a once-in-a-universe happening . . . totally unique . . . ODD.

But, over time, life has rubbed up against us, making many of us "Even." Perhaps you have concluded that being ODD—being true to yourself—is somehow negative or an ideal that you should long ago have abandoned. Perhaps the idea of being ODD may even seem a little scary.

Throughout our lives, we are *expected* to do things by society's standards. We are trained, early in life, how to think and how to fit in so that we may "succeed," as it is defined by the rest of the world.

We are all born with ODDITUDE. But then the vast majority

of us allowed our families, schools, friends, coworkers, and playmates to blunt the sharp edges of our spirits until all the ODD had been smoothed away, and we were all flat and even.

As my grandfather often said to me, "ODD is when you are true to yourself. 'Even' is when you are 'true' to the wishes of others at the expense of yourself." Then he would often add something that has truly made a difference in my life: "Being even is an expense because if you are not being yourself, how can you fully enjoy the journey of living? How can you be happy? How can you discover the true passion of your life—the reason you were put on this planet? How can you really love who you are and love what you do if you are not living as the real *you*?"

Ask yourself:

- ➡ Is my life overflowing with fun or frustration?
- ➡ Am I bubbling or bored?
- ➡ When I wake up in the morning, can I hardly wait to get started? Or can I hardly wait to be finished?
- ➡ At night, do I fall asleep with the exhaustion that comes from doing what I love? Or is my soul slowly being suffocated by a monotonous existence because I am only doing what others expect of me?

From now on, I will give you two ideas to think about at the end of each chapter. The first one will, hopefully, help you discover your own Wizard of ODD. The other will give you ideas about how you can become a Wizard of ODD to others. Of course, by being a wizard to others, you will also become a better wizard to yourself.

In addition, at the end of this book, I have included what I call "Charge Cards." These cards are designed to be cut out from this book and used in your daily life. Their purpose? Every day, most of us experience "transitional meltdowns," where we lose our spiritual momentum. These transitional meltdowns are usually triggered by a change in our physical environment or the time of the day. Common causes of transitional meltdowns include a long and difficult commute to work, returning to the workplace after lunch, late-afternoon fatigue, the commute home, and after-dinner drowsiness. By reading and thinking about the Charge Card you have chosen that day, you will recharge your spiritual batteries and move on to the next challenge with renewed enthusiasm.

An ODD View

BECOMING YOUR WIZARD OF ODD: Keep in mind that those who thirst for recognition from others don't recognize much in themselves.

BEING A WIZARD OF ODD TO OTHERS: Encourage those you care about to become their own wizards. Remind them that when they do, they will be:

- JOYOUS. They will love who they are and what they do.
- CREATIVE. They will learn from everyone around them, but they will live their lives in their own unique way.
- DEMANDING. They will settle for nothing less than the very best from both themselves and everyone around them.

They will be ODD.

My First Wizard of ODD

I was lucky. I had wonderful parents. They had an agreement that they'd never go to bed mad at one another. Made it rather tough on us kids. Not easy talking to someone who hasn't slept in fourteen years.

Okay, that's a joke. My parents were great—the original odd couple.

One of the nicest things about growing up in my house was that my grandfather lived with us. My grandfather was a teacher. He drove a bus for the city of Chicago, but he only did that for the money. . . . He was really a teacher. The most vital lesson he ever taught me was the importance, the excitement, the beauty, the challenge of being ODD.

If it was your second time on the bus, my grandfather knew your name, the name of your husband or wife, your children, where you worked, and where you lived. He knew you. People would actually pass up other buses to get on his bus, because it was like a moving party. I've had people come up to me thirty years later and say, "I remember your grandfather. I used to ride on his bus. He was the highlight of my day."

Wow. *The highlight of my day.* What a wonderful way to be remembered, and here's a man with whom they'd spent only a few moments. How is it that he made such an impact on people? Because he was ODD. He believed that life is a gift, and, as a gift, it's meant to be enjoyed and not just endured.

We are all teachers all the time especially when we are around young minds. I learned that a number of years ago when my daughter was three. One morning, I planned on walking to the cleaners, which was just a block away. But when I reached the back porch, I saw that it was raining. My wife's car was in the driveway, so I thought I'd borrow it.

But I must have lost my mind momentarily, because I did not ask her permission first. I just presumed she wasn't going anywhere in the next seventy-five seconds.

Sure enough, when I pulled back into the driveway, there was my wife standing on the back porch. Her arms were folded, and her foot was tapping. My three-year-old daughter was standing next to her. Her arms were folded. Her foot was tapping. As I got out of the car, my daughter sweetly said to me, "Daddy, did it ever occur to you to take your own damn car?"

❊

Sitting at the kitchen table with my grandfather one afternoon. We were beginning to put together a new jigsaw puzzle. I was ten years old. I remember all the irregular pieces spread out in front of us as we started to sort them into similar colors and patterns. He asked me, "You know what I love about puzzles?" I shook my head, more interested in solving the puzzle. He held up a piece. "Each one of these is different. But put them all together in just the right way and they make a wonderful picture.

"Same is true of people. Each one of us is different—ODD—and yet, if we are true to ourselves we all manage to fit together perfectly. If any two pieces are alike, you no longer have a puzzle that is a beautiful picture waiting to happen. You just have a pile of useless pieces."

Looking back, I realize my grandfather's strongest belief was that in a world of Evens, you had to be ODD. To my grandfather, "ODD" was not a negative word—just the opposite. He understood that trying to be like everyone else was poison. He believed that he and I and everyone else on this planet was one of a kind. In order to live a happy life, you had to first be true to yourself. He would often say, "Look within you and discover your Wizard of ODD."

My grandfather and his belief in ODDITUDE gave him a lust for living that enveloped everyone around him. There was an honesty about him that made people feel excited about being alive. You wanted to be around my grandfather because, when you were, you felt better about life. You felt better about yourself.

My grandfather was a very religious man. One day, when my brother and I were in our teens, acting like jerks, he sat us down at the kitchen table and took out the Bible. My grandfather said, "The beauty of the scriptures is not so much what is written but what is read." He then read the passage where Abraham is asked to sacrifice his son, Isaac. When my grandfather finished reading, he commented, "Now, if you know how to read the scriptures, you realize that Isaac was twelve years old or younger."

I asked, "Where does it say that?"

"Well," said my grandfather, "if he had been a teenager, then it wouldn't have been a sacrifice."

My grandfather believed in living a life of total joy—loving who you are; loving what you do. He would often say, "Do what you love, and you'll be known as a smart person. But, sometimes, life doesn't give you that opportunity. Then you must learn to love what you do, and you'll be known as a wise person. But if you can do neither—if you can't do what you love or learn to love what you do—then do something else. Life is too precious to waste even a moment of it."

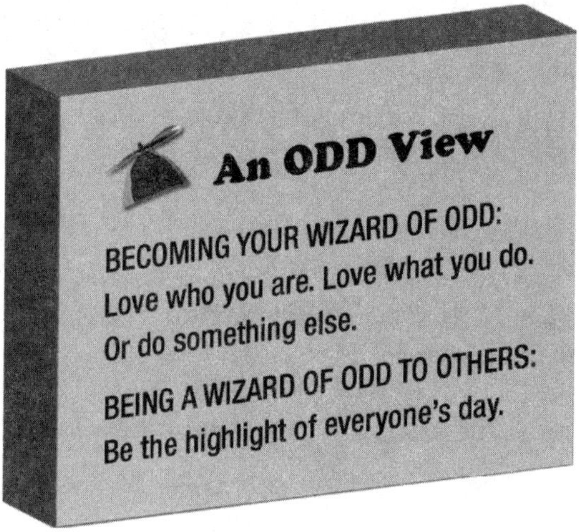
An ODD View
BECOMING YOUR WIZARD OF ODD:
Love who you are. Love what you do.
Or do something else.
BEING A WIZARD OF ODD TO OTHERS:
Be the highlight of everyone's day.

My Journey from Even to ODD

The first few miles of my life were a bumpy road. I was a very unpopular child. When I was four years old, some neighborhood kids tied me to a tree. Two years later, my parents came looking for me. Three years later, they untied me.

In my neighborhood, sports were important. I was a horrible athlete. On my Little League team, for instance, I did not get to actually play until the last game of the season. I asked the coach why I was batting ninth. He said, "Because there is no tenth."

Academically, the only thing that made my grades in elementary school look pretty darn good were the grades I got in high school. I graduated in the bottom 3 percent of my high school class.

Fortunately, previous success of any kind is not a prerequisite for living a life of happiness. I just had to start accepting myself for who I was. Only when I truly became a student of life did I realize that the road to being faithful to myself could have begun much earlier had I listened to the real teachers I met every day and who were trying to teach me the lessons of life.

These teachers enriched my spirit and helped me to discover who I really am and what I really want to do. I was given extraordinary wisdom from "ordinary" people. . . .

My grandfather as we sat on the stoop
My great aunt Rita who lived next door
Mom in the kitchen
Dad while he was working on the car
Neighbors who walked by my house
Friends
Strangers
Lovers
Allies
Enemies
Teachers
Students
Kids I grew up with
Children I raised and who raised me

Slowly, I "zigged" and "zagged" toward my ODD. Today, I am a professional speaker and writer. I love what I do.

Finding and living your ODD has nothing to do with how old you are now and everything to do with how young you want to feel. Bill was fifty-five years old. He had just retired after working thirty years at a job he hated. He told me, "I've always wanted to be an attorney, but I guess I'm too old now."

I asked Bill how long it would take him to go through law school. He replied, "I figure that the longest it would take me would be about five years."

I asked him how old he would be in five years.

He said, "Sixty."

"If you don't go to law school, how old will you be in five years?"

Bill had a choice. He could either spend the next five years joyously pursuing his dream or merely enduring those years as he had the past thirty-five. He could be ODD or Even.

I have a friend, Kate, who is eighty-one. She is young, packing every moment with energy, excitement, and passion for who she is and what she does. ODD.

I have another friend, Chad, who is already very old at nineteen. He literally dreads the morning light. His existence is soaked with boredom, frustration, and depression because he is living his life according to the opinions of those around him.

This book will help you discover who you are and what you really want to do. But mostly, it will enable you to understand the idea of ODDITUDE, enabling you to enhance your uniqueness and to release an emotional energy that will transform your existence into the life you long to live.

An ODD View

BECOMING YOUR WIZARD OF ODD: To be ODD, you must develop spiritual muscles, the strength to stand alone and the will to rule your world.

BEING A WIZARD OF ODD TO OTHERS: As you know, today's world is more than just you—it is also the art of leadership and teamwork, effectively communicating with others, dealing with change, problem solving, and creative thinking. Someone once said, "No man is an island." Of course, no man is a couch either. But that's not the point. The point is that we must learn to effectively interact and cooperate with others.

Northern California's giant redwoods are among the oldest living organisms on the planet, having survived over two thousand years of storms. People simply presume these trees have deep roots. In fact, they are surrounded by sandy soil and have shallow roots. But their roots interlock with other nearby redwoods, which is what gives them all the strength to survive.

Being ODD Will Give You What You Deserve

. . . A world far beyond what you can now imagine.

There are motivational "experts" who will tell you that you can be *anything* you want to be. You already know that statement's a lie. Those "experts" are idiots. If you are five-two, three hundred pounds, and forty-one years old, you are not going to be a Rockette. Get used to the idea.

You cannot be *anything* you want to be, but you can be far more than you ever imagined. You deserve that. You're ODD.

If you relish the reality that you are ODD, your spirit will sizzle with passion. You will discover, dwell on, and develop what makes you special. Your life will become an endless celebration of, determination for, and belief in the ideals that define you, the feelings that fill you, and the dreams that drive you.

Your ODD will silence all those who say you can't do it, you shouldn't do it, or you won't do it, because they will soon realize their opinion is irrelevant to you.

ODD will erase your self-doubt and fill your heart with love for who you are and what you do.

When you have ODDITUDE, you:

- ➡ Realize that time always passes too quickly
- ➡ Are totally in the moment
- ➡ Don't let the means become the end
- ➡ Enrich the lives of those around you
- ➡ Don't envy others
- ➡ Are always trying to become better
- ➡ Believe that money is a factor, not the final evaluation
- ➡ Know that passion is the heartbeat of an ODD person

Sometimes, many times, you do what you need to do rather than what you want to do. When I was in high school, I got a job as a busboy at a big restaurant. I could have asked my parents for money, but, even then, I realized they didn't have much of it. Besides, I liked the independence I felt when my work put a few bucks into my own pocket. But I had not yet learned ODDITUDE. I broke every one of the statements listed above.

Each minute I worked took an hour to go by. I was never in the moment and was always thinking of anything but what I was doing. The end was removing dirty dishes and cleaning up the tables. But the means, my hourly wage, was all I was concerned with. I really didn't care if I was enriching the lives of those around me. Envy? I recall thinking one day as I was leaving my house that the dog was leading a more rewarding life than I was. Not a good sign. I was never trying to become better.

The money, not the job, was all I cared about. I had not yet learned that passion is the heartbeat of ODDITUDE. My grandfather's words had been forgotten. "Do what you love *or* learn to love what you do *or* do something else." Eventually, I was fired and deservedly so.

Today, my daughters tease me about my not being able to cook. But I tell them that I am such a brilliant "cleaner-upper" that I can always find someone who cooks. When I am cleaning up after a big meal, am I passionate about it? Yes. I have learned to love it. I tell myself that I want to do it rather than that I need to do it. Also, I focus on the positive elements of tidying up. For instance, clean dishes live far longer than cooked meals.

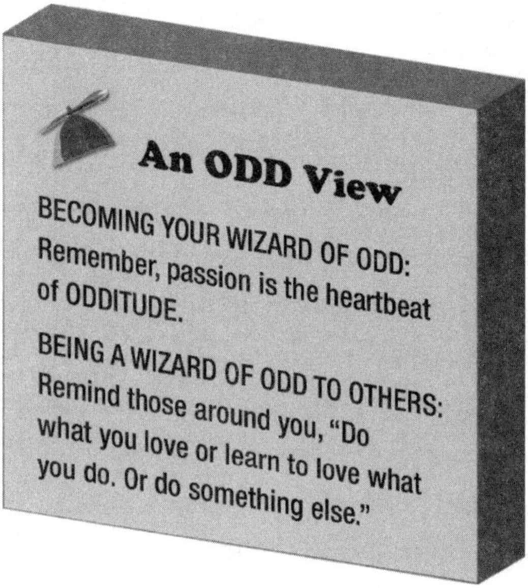
An ODD View
BECOMING YOUR WIZARD OF ODD:
Remember, passion is the heartbeat of ODDITUDE.
BEING A WIZARD OF ODD TO OTHERS:
Remind those around you, "Do what you love or learn to love what you do. Or do something else."

There Is a First Time and a Last Time for Everything

One of the things my grandfather taught me as we sat on our front porch watching the world walk by is that there is a first time and a last time for everything. He would say, "When you sit down to dinner, look at those faces around you and cherish that moment because there was a first time and there will surely be a last."

We all get up on certain mornings feeling like we just don't want to go through the day that's ahead of us. But if we are on this planet long enough, we'd give anything to live that day again.

You hear people say it all the time: "Oh, I'm just too busy. I have so many things to do."

The next time "busy" becomes a burden, go to a nursing home. Hang around with some people who have nothing to do all day. "Busy" will look good.

Years ago, I got a call from a theatrical producer who asked me to work on a project that would require me to be away from home for about six months. "Can't do it," I replied.

"Why not?" he asked.

"Because I have a daughter who is about to turn four. She is going to be four for exactly three hundred and sixty-five days whether I'm there or not."

One of the great lessons that children teach us is the immediacy of "now."

So many of us spend time reliving the past or worrying about the future that all those little pieces called "now" go by virtually unnoticed. Evens do not realize that the supply of "now" is limited. ODDs do.

When I was a young man and my brother was younger, I was sitting in the living room doing something. . . . I can't remember what. He was going out the door to his part-time job at the grocery store. He said good-bye, and I replied likewise. I never spoke to him again because he died a few hours later in an accident. There is a first time and a last time for everything.

An ODD View

BECOMING YOUR WIZARD OF ODD: Remind yourself that every moment on this planet is a privilege. Live passionately. Have fun. Be ODD. Now.

BEING A WIZARD OF ODD TO OTHERS: Remember, the time you share with someone is a once-in-a-lifetime opportunity. How would you treat that person if you knew you would never see him or her again?

Never Walk a Road That Doesn't Lead to Your Heart

Sister Lee was the most vicious, violent, intimidating human being I have ever known. She was three feet tall and getting shorter every year. On the day I started eighth grade, she was about a billion years old. At that time, the Catholic schools had a rather unique retirement system. It was called death.

We children feared Sister Lee more than we feared God. We believed in God. We had met Sister Lee.

She was a legend among us kids. To this day, you can go into my old neighborhood, walk into a tavern, step up to the bar, and announce, "Sister Lee taught me eighth grade," and people will begin buying you drinks.

Sister Lee's tests consisted of answers. You had to provide the questions. The only ones marked wrong were those you could not explain.

When I first walked into my eighth-grade classroom, I expected to see autumn leaves on the bulletin board or cutouts of children playing on swings. Not Sister Lee. She believed in the power of words.

On her bulletin board, the very first day, were the words, "Discipline is remembering what I want." Every week, there would be a new aphorism. I don't remember all of them, but a couple of the others were "Idiocy is doing the same thing over and over and expecting different results," and "The Lord's coming. Look busy."

During the school day, Sister Lee might point to a saying on the bulletin board and asked one of us how those words were enriching our life. If we could not give a good answer, our life might come to a sudden and abrupt end.

Sister Lee never raised her voice. She never had to. You did not want to annoy her. No one ever did it twice.

Each aphorism spent a week up on the bulletin board except for the last one, which went up there in mid-April and stayed until the end of the school year: "Never walk a road that doesn't lead to your heart."

The last day of eighth grade: The books had been collected, and the papers had been turned in. We were sitting at our desks just running out the clock. A student asked Sister Lee, "Sister, why do we have to go to school?" That was a very bold question to present to a nun, particularly this one. We held our breath, fearing a final explosion.

Sister Lee thought about it a moment and then replied, "I don't know the purpose of school. But I do know the purpose of education. It's to set you free . . ." She pointed to the phrase on the bulletin board. ". . . so you can walk the road that leads to your heart."

Sister Lee was the kind of teacher that, as a kid, when you saw her walking down the street, you would go blocks out of your way to avoid saying hello. But when you grew up and came back, she was the very first person you looked for.

After I had written my first novel, I drove back to the old neighborhood and parked across the street from the school. At three o'clock, the kids came out. A little while later, all the teachers but Sister Lee came out. As the neighborhood was growing dark, the door creaked opened and out hobbled Sister Lee.

She must have been 5 billion years old by then and an inch-and-a-half tall.

I walked up to her. "Sister Lee, do you remember me?"

She stared up.

"I'm John Powers. You taught me eighth grade."

Finally, she smiled. "Oh, yes . . . John Powers. I'm sorry. All grades are final."

I know why she lived so long. God's no fool. He didn't want to deal with Sister Lee either.

Sister Lee taught me that if I choose the road that leads to my heart, I will always live a life of ODDITUDE.

An ODD View

BECOMING YOUR WIZARD OF ODD. Never walk a road that doesn't lead to your heart. Remember, idiocy is doing the same thing over and over and expecting different results.

BEING A WIZARD OF ODD TO OTHERS: Help others find the path that is meant for them. When you do, the road to your own heart will be that much easier to find.

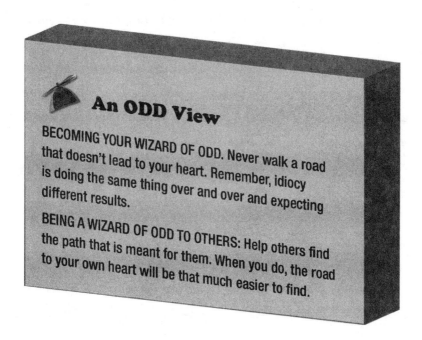

The World Is Filled with Unfulfilled People

. . . but why should you be one of them? Walk down any street, ride any bus, stand in any room, and look at the faces around you. Too often, bored, tired, stressed, and unhappy expressions look back. Indifference drips from their souls.

When you discover, live, and nurture your ODD, you enrich the lives of everyone around you, too. After all, how can you instill passion in others when there is no passion within you? How can you love others when you don't love yourself? How can you inspire and lead others when you yourself don't know where you're going? How can you inspire change in others when your own spirit is shackled by mediocrity? You cannot give what you have not got.

If you haven't committed a crime, then you shouldn't be in jail. But so often, we allow our spirits to be locked in cells surrounded by bars we ourselves have created—bars of guilt, fear, boredom, anxiety, frustration, anger, and depression. When you fill your heart with ODD for who you are, what you do, and where you want to go, those bars melt away.

We waste so much time trying to be like everyone else and worrying about what others think of us.

Many people, it seems, have yet to, and will never, come anywhere near completely unwrapping this gift of life. Because they refuse to accept how unique and ODD they are, they will leave this earth without traveling to the outer limits of their universe. They will not experience all the joy their spirit deserves.

Look at Kate, my "older" friend. When life excites her, and it often does, she throws up her arms and yells her favorite word, "Hurray!" Doesn't matter where she is—someone's living room, a Laundromat, a library. . . . At such times, adults think she's crazy. But I have noticed that when young children are around, they throw up their arms and shout, "Hurray," too.

I once asked her why she did that. She said, "Because it feels so good."

I tried it. She's right. Hurray!

An ODD View

BECOMING YOUR WIZARD OF ODD: This book is not about you being like everyone else. It's about you living *your* life your way, loving who you are, loving what you do. Remind yourself, "I am on a lifelong journey to discover this universe called 'Me.'" You haven't committed a crime, so get out of jail.

BEING A WIZARD OF ODD TO OTHERS: Do you know people who are walking around in a virtual coma? Are they merely going through the motions of living? When you help them discover what makes them ODD, you will fuel your own fire for who you are and what you do. Hurray!

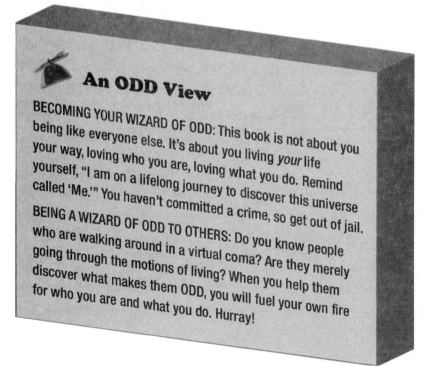

Mom Was an ODD Lady . . .

It takes courage to be ODD. Courage is contagious. Mom was a carrier. She was far from perfect but closer than most of us will ever get.

Mom was one tough lady. She had to be. She was raised by my grandmother. Because of my grandmother, my mother was highly neurotic. Because of my mother, I'm no slice of sunshine either.

Mom always had the courage to say what she felt had to be said or do what she believed had to be done. She never shrank from challenging the conventional thinking of those around her.

Like my grandfather, my father's father, my mother loved to sit on the front steps, too. She used to say, "The world would be a better place if there were fewer air conditioners and more front porches."

There were many terms used to describe my grandmother: "Difficult," "disagreeable," "unpredictable," "mean," "moody" . . .

but the one that finally stuck, sadly enough, was "mentally ill." My grandmother spent the last twenty-eight years of her life in a state mental hospital.

During those twenty-eight years, every other Saturday, Mom would drive to visit my grandmother. Three hours there and three hours back. My dad had to work weekends, so she always made the trip alone.

I remember when I was sixteen years old—an age when you're willing to drive anyone anywhere just to get behind the wheel. One Saturday morning, I offered to drive Mom to the hospita, l and she accepted.

I had seen my grandmother about six years earlier, before she had been committed. But the old lady that Mom sat down and tried to talk to neither looked nor sounded anything like the woman I had known. And she had no idea who we were.

At first, my grandmother thought I was my mother's boyfriend. A few moments later, she had forgotten that. Then, my grandmother thought we were neighbors she had known many years ago. So it went. At one point, my grandmother warned me not to talk to anyone on the third floor. There was no third floor. The entire "visit" lasted fewer than twenty minutes.

Driving home, I asked Mom, "What's the point? All this time, all this effort, and she doesn't even know who you are."

Mom said, "I don't go there because she knows who I am. I go there because I want the doctors, the nurses, every one of the staff, and all the other patients to know that my mother is somebody. She is loved and she is being watched."

During the rest of the ride home, Mom told me about the last time my grandmother had been committed. On a bitterly cold January day, Mom had gone over to my grandmother's house, which was completely shuttered. When my grandmother finally answered the door, she was wearing a heavy winter coat and explained that there were five thousand marines in the basement trying to come up through the heating vents to get her. So my grandmother had shut off all the heat.

My mother said to me, "The poor women truly believed it. You could see it in her eyes. She was terrified."

Mom had to call both the fire department and the police department, who then had to break down the door to get my grandmother out of the house.

Mom had a strange sense of humor. She said to me, "Five thousand marines. I went down into that basement. There couldn't have been more than three hundred."

Mom was an only child. Too bad. She could have used some allies. When Mom was ten months old, her real father left the family. About a year later, my grandmother married a very nice man named Jim. He was too nice. Jim either wouldn't or couldn't protect my mother from her mother. As the years went by and my grandmother's mind deteriorated, only two people stuck with her: Jim, who suffered in silence, and my mother, who suffered at the top of her lungs.

Sometimes, you do not understand a book until the last page has been read. As I've said, Mom was one tough lady and that's how everyone treated her, including my dad and me. Only looking back, after she was gone, did I wonder how she felt when the main man in her life deserted her at that cutie-pie, totally innocent age of ten months?

Only then did I wonder how she viewed all men when the first one in her life left her and the second one refused to protect her.

Only then did I realize I had never offered her what she always craved and never got—the totally unconditional love of a father. The kind of love that says, "I will protect you from the dragons," "You are the center of my universe," "It's just you and me, kid." That kind of love.

Only then did I wish I could sit down and just listen to my mother talk. No matter what she said, I would reply, "You're right, Mom. You are absolutely right." Not that I would have treated her that way all the time. But, sometimes, surely, sometimes.

Sometimes—no—all the time, it takes more courage than most of us possess to truly understand the people who are closest to us.

An ODD View

BECOMING YOUR WIZARD OF ODD: Evens go with the flow. ODDS have the courage to ride the waves.

BEING A WIZARD OF ODD TO OTHERS: Courage is contagious. When you live it, those around you will eventually learn it.

Time to Boogie

If you don't revel in who you are and what you do, what's the alternative? Plodding through life with blinders on so you don't get too depressed by seeing what you're missing? Want to know the feeling? Talk to a plow horse—the two-legged kind.

In the play *The Traveling Girl,* an older, lonely woman hears music coming from the town dance hall. She stands in the street and says to no one in particular, except to herself, "If I had my life to live over, I'd learn to dance. I swear my whole life would have been different if only I had learned how to dance."

When your spirit dances, you are living a life of ODD.

An ODD View

BECOMING YOUR WIZARD OF ODD:
Time to boogie.

BEING A WIZARD OF ODD TO OTHERS:
Teach others to boogie, too. There's a time and a place to dance alone. But, usually, it's a lot more fun when everyone dances together.

From the Sun to the Moon

Even days are quickly forgotten. It is the ODD ones we remember.

"Daddy, what do you remember about being eleven?"

The question is being asked by my daughter who just happens to be eleven but only for a few more days. Twelve is waiting for her at the end of the week.

We are sitting at the kitchen table on a Saturday night looking through an astronomy magazine that is written for kids. Astronomy is one of her many passions.

It is a summer evening. A breeze occasionally drifts in through the screen door, and the night is beginning to run across the sky.

"Not much," I confess. "I remember trying to jump over a park bench and getting four stitches in my knee. For whatever reason, I recall sitting on the curb outside of Drexel's Drugstore and sharing a pint of chocolate ice cream with Bobby Hrad. That's about it."

"That's all you remember?"

"'Fraid so."

"Daddy, I'm only going to be eleven for a few more days!"

"I'm aware of that."

"I want to do something while I'm still eleven that I'll remember for the rest of my life."

"Well," I say, "I could run you over with the car a few times. If I can still recall trying to jump over a park bench, you'd certainly remember that."

She gives me that slight rolling of the eyes and a big sigh, her eleven-year-old way of dismissing inane remarks. No man is a prophet in his own land or a comedian in his own kitchen.

She goes back to flipping through the pages of the astronomy magazine. "There's an article in here that says within the next fifty years the average person will be able to visit the moon. It would be so cool if I could do it right now. You never forget something like that."

Suddenly, her head snaps up and she looks at me, excitement flashing all over her face. "I know what we can do. We can walk around the lake."

We live directly across the street from either a very large, small lake or a very small, large lake. A twenty-seven-mile path, which by state law is public access, runs completely around it. Parts of the path are very rough. I have been told that it takes at least twelve hours of brisk walking to go completely around it.

I'm about to respond to my daughter with a litany of excuses: I have work to do. It's supposed to rain tomorrow. You'd never be able to walk that far. Your room's a mess and you have to clean it up first.

But she is eleven. Like most parents of a child that age, I know the days she will want to spend with me are quickly diminishing.

"We'll have to get up very early," I warn her.

"That's fine with me."

"We'll have to walk all day and into the night."

"I know."

The next morning, with the sun's forehead peeking over the trees, my daughter and I, along with a few neighbors, begin our first steps on the path. I don't tell my neighbors what she plans on doing. If she changes her mind, and I suspect she will, she won't feel like a quitter in their eyes.

The morning walk is a pleasant one, and it brings us into another town on the lake. But the next two hours take their toll on everyone. We have now walked a total of five hours with only a short break. The lone remaining neighbor has clearly had it and has called a friend to come and pick him up. I suggest to my daughter that we take the ride home, too.

"No," she says defiantly. "I can do it. I know I can. Why? Are you getting tired?"

"I can make it," I assure her. "But let me explain a few things. We have only walked about five hours. To make it the rest of the way is going to take anywhere from seven to nine more hours. The next town we reach will be ours. From here on in, there's no way we'll be able to call for a ride."

She says it again. "I can do it."

I don't think she can, and I have no desire to be caught out in the middle of nowhere with a child who cannot take another step. But, hey, I have a sense of history, too.

Minutes later, we are walking beneath some weeping willows with branches so thick that only a few drops of sunlight can trickle through. "You know," I say to her, "you and I, just the two of us, will probably never again take a walk together as long as this one."

"Cool," she says.

I agree. "Cool."

For the next couple of hours, the conversation is constant. But the passing miles slowly extinguish our words. She is really starting to tire, and I wonder how we're going to get home.

A particularly long stretch of silence grows up between us.

"Tired?" I ask.

"A little," she says as she picks up a stripped branch and begins using it as a walking stick. "But I never want to forget this day so my memory is taking notes."

As the fading sunlight settles on the earth, we manage to accidentally walk into a small swamp, which engulfs our feet in mud.

A few minutes later, it is completely dark. We are walking along a highway that skirts the lake for about a block. A full moon and clear night look down on us. We are about to enter the final, and toughest, part of the walk. At the other end of these few miles of slippery hills lay the beginning of our town. At that point, we'll only be a few blocks from home.

We step off the highway and onto the base of the first hill. "Stay right behind me," I tell her and she does.

It's a slugfest. Tree branches throw uppercuts, quick jabs, and roundhouse curves. Bushes fire low punches, and tree stumps try to knock us down. A short, lone fence post catches me right above the knee and sends me reeling, but I stay on my feet. My daughter just laughs. There are moments when the fight is at a standstill. But slowly, inevitably, we move forward.

We have just crawled up a half-eaten stairway that was hidden in the side of a hill when we feel something strange under our feet. Grass. We look up and realize that we are on someone's front lawn. We're in town.

The victory march begins. Our eyes, so accustomed to darkness, flinch at the rawness of the town's glare. But every street light, every neon sign, every stranger walking by is, in our imaginations, part of the mob that worships us. We congratulate each other dozens of times. Walking down the street, we are giddy with the laughter that is the wreath of winners.

She is too excited to sleep, so we sit on the front porch swing, looking out at the black water of the lake. I'm afraid she'll really be hurting in the morning, but, in fact, she will pop out of bed while it will be three days before I'm walking normally again.

My daughter looks up at the clear sky. "You know, Daddy, we started with the Sun and ended with the Moon."

"So we did."

"Fifty years from now, if I ever do walk on the moon, I'll probably be part of a tour group. I don't think I'll ever discover a new star. But not many people can say they walked from the Sun to the Moon."

"No, not many."

An ODD View
BECOMING YOUR WIZARD OF ODD:
Try to make every day an ODD one.
BEING A WIZARD TO OTHERS:
Help them live ODD days, too.

Love-a-holic or Work-a-holic

Loving your ODD is the difference between a "work-a-holic," who puts all of their time into their job, and a "love-a-holic," who puts all of their creativity, humanity, common sense, and intellect into their career. Love-a-holics always do better than work-a-holics because we are all better at playing than working. Playing is a more natural activity. That's why, when children get up in the morning, they look for toys, not the want ads.

Ever come home from work so tired you can hardly move? The phone rings. One of your favorite friends calls and invites you to dinner or a movie or a great party. Often, your spirit is flooded with renewed energy. You are ready to play.

Playing is like dessert. There's always room for it.

A friend of mine is a surgeon who pursues his profession six days a week, fourteen hours a day. But he told me, "The only time I 'work' is on Sunday when I play golf with my wife. I hate golf. But I love my wife . . . and performing surgeries."

Work is anything you don't want to do. When you live a life that truly reflects who you are and what you really want to do, you'll never work a day in your life.

Isn't that the whole idea? To have more fun doing what you love to do?

An ODD View

BECOMING YOUR WIZARD OF ODD: If you're going to "work" every morning, something's wrong.

BEING A WIZARD OF ODD TO OTHERS: Ask yourself and the others in your organization, are you a love-a-holic or a work-a-holic? In a business situation, if all of you are playing and your competition is working, who do you think is going to win?

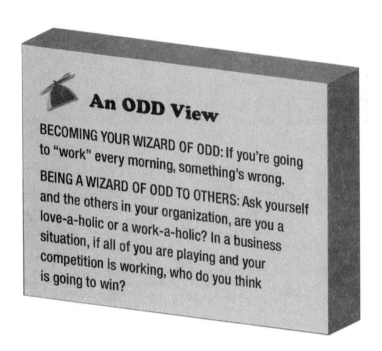

Hide-and-Seek

My daughter never particularly liked sports. But she loved games. When she was a few months old, she became a world-class peek-a-boo player. By the time she was three, she was playing the real thing, hide-and-seek.

One morning, she came into the kitchen and asked me if I'd like to play a game of hide-and-seek.

I asked her, "You know how?"

She said, "Mostly. I've watched the older kids down the block. Now you start counting, and before I leave, I'll tell you where I'm hiding."

"No," I said. "That's not how you do it. You hide and then I try to find you."

She sighed. "How are you going to find me if I don't tell you where I am?"

Only three years old and already she realized I was in over my head.

"Look," I said emphatically, "I'll count and you hide."

I was on *seven* when I heard her voice from the closet.

"Ready."

I spent a few moments "looking" for her, and then I opened the closet door. There she stood, grinning, giggling, and jiggling just from the sheer anticipation of being discovered.

Every time we played the game, she became just a little harder to find.

Actually, we had not played hide-and-seek for quite a while when she came into my office one night and asked me if I'd like to play. "Sure," I said. "I'll count to ten . . ."

"No," she interrupted, "I'll do the counting. You do the hiding." She was a first grader now and very proud of knowing her numbers.

As she began counting, I went and crouched under my desk. Not a good choice. Immediately, I could hear my knees screaming at me. But I figured I could last until she counted to ten. The new first grader counted to one hundred and thirty-eight before I finally heard her say, "Ready or not, here I come."

❊

I knew the day would arrive, and it did. One afternoon, I asked her if she'd like to play a game of hide-and-seek.

"Dad, I'm too old for that."

Hardly. When she became a teenager, the real game of hide-and-seek began. At times, she'd hide her thoughts, her friends, her feelings, where she was going, or what she was doing. All the time, I'd be seeking, trying to figure out what the heck was going on. While I was seeking her, she was seeking the rest of the world: seeking new ideas, new thoughts, new friends, and new feelings. In a million ways she was saying, "Dad, here's the grown-up me. Ready or not, here I come."

Of course, as she gets older, like all of us, she'll have to make a choice: to live a life of either hiding or seeking. Will she hide from the excitement of life or seek it?

Will she hide from the tough choices or seek them? Will she hide from hard work or seek it? Most important, will she hide from the dangers of true love or seek it?

I can only hope I've taught her well because every day the world will shout at her, "Ready or not, here I come!"

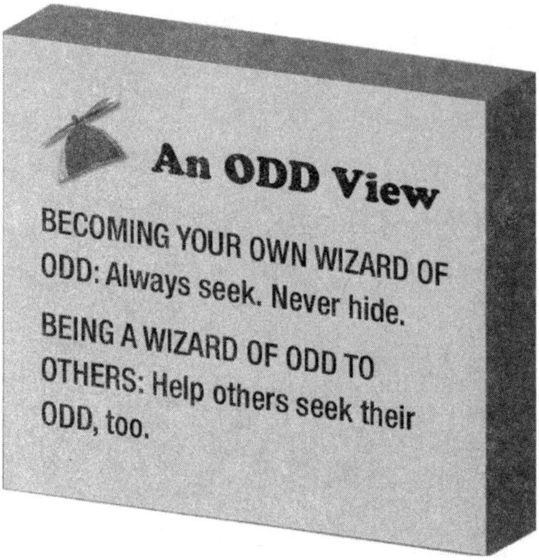
An ODD View
BECOMING YOUR OWN WIZARD OF ODD: Always seek. Never hide.
BEING A WIZARD OF ODD TO OTHERS: Help others seek their ODD, too.

Without ODD, There Is No Sense of Direction

A fellow went to the airport, walked up to the counter, and asked the agent for a ticket.

"What is your destination?" asked the agent.

"Oh, I don't know," replied the fellow. "I'd just like to go somewhere."

"Fine, but where?"

"Somewhere," said the fellow. "I just want to go somewhere. Doesn't matter."

The ticket agent thought he was crazy. Not surprising. But so many people do the same thing with their lives that it's considered normal. In fact, such people are not going "somewhere" at all. They are going nowhere.

An ODD View

BECOMING YOUR WIZARD OF ODD: Remember, the trouble with going nowhere is that it takes forever to get there. When you are not true to yourself, when you do not live your ODD, there is no sense of direction. There is no purpose.

BEING A WIZARD OF ODD TO OTHERS: Are there people in your life who seem to be going nowhere? Ask them if they have a destination. Just having the question put to them may motivate them to think about it and ask themselves, "What makes me special? What makes me ODD?"

Bet You Know What You *Don't* Want to Do

ODDS know what they want . . . or don't want.

A friend of mine asked, "How can I discover what I want to do if I don't even know what I want to do?"

"Easy," I replied. "I bet you know what you don't want to do."

He certainly did.

Sometimes, the first step in finding what makes you special, awakening your ODD, is being determined to change your current situation.

Perhaps you are dissatisfied with your present job so you start looking around for new opportunities. You live in an area of the country you don't like so you begin researching other areas. You're physically out of shape and don't like the way you feel, so you start an exercise program. You're not as thrilled about getting into good shape as you are passionate about getting out of bad shape.

Great start!

An example from my own life: As I mentioned earlier, I was a horrible student. Graduating from high school, I didn't know what I wanted to do with my life. But I certainly knew what I didn't want to do: work for a living.

I grew up on the South Side of Chicago. "Work" often meant picking up heavy objects in one place and moving them to another. All day. Boring. Or getting a low-paying office job shuffling papers all day. Also boring.

My high school guidance counselor, having reviewed my "permanent records," suggested that I learn a trade. I'm stupid but not that stupid. "Trade" is just another word for work.

*

A number of years ago, I bought a house. The day after moving in, I stopped to talk to my new neighbor, who was sweeping out his garage. I mentioned that I was thinking of buying a chainsaw.

He said, "I've known you for less than ten minutes. But I already know that, if you do, you're going to kill yourself with it."

He handed me his hedge clippers. "See if you can survive with these first."

He was right. Within a few minutes, I almost cut off the tip of my finger.

I have great admiration for people in the trades, such as carpenters, plumbers, and electricians. One reason is that I could never begin to do any of their jobs. I'm a total klutz. I simply don't have the brains for that kind of talent.

My parents had always told me I was going to college. Apparently, they realized, long before I did, that education was the only life preserver in the water for me. So it wasn't a case of my wanting to go to college as much as it was of my really not wanting to go anywhere else.

I applied to and was rejected by thirty-five different colleges and universities. One school's letter of rejection contained only two words, "You're kidding!"

I was finally accepted by Loyola University of Chicago, which at that time, would accept just about anyone and then quickly flunk them out if they didn't produce. Thank you, Loyola University.

My parents had lots of love. Not much money. Although I lived at home and ate their food, tuition was my problem.

The campus I attended at Loyola was located in downtown Chicago. Every day, I traveled an hour and a half, each way, by bus and elevated train, to attend classes. After school, I'd work four hours at various part-time jobs. During the summers, I worked full-time at the very jobs—construction, factory work, and low-level office jobs—that I was going to college to avoid.

After three months of that, I couldn't wait to get back to school. I wasn't as much filled with the desire of wanting to learn as I was filled with the desire of not wanting to flunk out because I knew the fate that awaited me if I did: work.

All my friends were on full or partial scholarships, so I did indeed pay for screwing up in high school.

Eventually, I earned my Ph.D. from Northwestern University, which created many options for my future. Among those options, I discovered what I love to do: teaching, writing, and professional speaking.

By the way, all of those letters of rejection didn't go to waste. A few years after I graduated, I was a professor at a state university in Illinois. I framed and hung some of the more amusing letters of rejection on my office wall.

Years after I left the university, I had a number of former students come up and tell me basically the same story, which was, "I came to your office to tell you I was dropping out of school. But after reading those letters, I figured that if a moron like you could get through college, so could I."

Sometimes, to find your ODD, you must force your mind and body to go where they haven't been before—think new thoughts, travel to new places. Exploring the world can be a very fun part of discovering your uniqueness.

If you don't know what you want, set sail from your current, unhappy situation to the open sea of possibilities. Eventually, and much sooner than you think, you will discover your new land of opportunity.

An ODD View

BECOMING YOUR WIZARD OF ODD: Be determined about wanting to change, about finding your ODD.

BEING A WIZARD OF ODD TO OTHERS: You know others in similar situations. Relate your experiences. When you share, you always get smarter. It cannot be otherwise. The new insights you acquire helping others will help you discover your own uniqueness that much sooner.

Theodore Derby, Another ODD Fellow

There's a toy box in a corner of my office that reminds me of Theodore Derby. Sometimes, when my daughter was small, she would come up to my office, take a toy out, and play with it for a while. When she got bored, she would take out another toy and play with that one for a while until she got bored with it, too. Eventually, she would get tired of the whole scene and leave the office, while the toys she had deserted would now be scattered all over the floor.

If I had been a strict parent, which I was not, I would have told her that she could not leave until she had put all her toys away. Sometimes, I did, but not very often. The truth is that I liked to have her visit, and I didn't want her to identify those visits with my nagging. I rationalized it by telling myself that when I went to parties, the host had to clean up after me. Whatever.

Putting the toys back in the box was when I thought about Theodore Derby.

I went to an all-boy high school. Every year we had a variety show. We were not an easy audience. We sixteen hundred boys were a sea of perpetual motion: bumping shoulders, scratching heads and crotches, cracking knuckles, shifting weight from one butt cheek to the other, belching, burping, and . . . worse.

The year I saw Theodore Derby perform, the first few acts of the variety show were the usual fare: a group from the band played a musical number, a few guys re-created a scene from some play, and a quartet sang "Oklahoma." Then Mr. Dremond from the drama department announced: "Theodore Derby will now sing a song he has written himself called, 'Love Looks So Much Like You.'"

Most of the guys were probably thinking like me: *What kind of moron sings a love song in front of sixteen hundred morons like us?*

Theodore's first words walked out slowly wrapped in a low, lazy velvet. Then, gradually, they lyrically strolled into a tenor's stride. "Maybe you're not the only girl for me. But when I look at love, yours is the only face I see."

As Theodore Derby continued to sing, every guy in the audience began thinking about the girl he had just fallen in love with or the one he was about to.

Theodore Derby's voice plummeted to barely a whisper as he sang the last words of his song. "Until my life is through, every beautiful song I hear will draw within my heart a memory of you."

Each of us sixteen hundred guys instinctively stood and applauded. Theodore Derby took a few bows, but he seemed neither surprised nor elated by the response.

The next morning at the bus stop, I told Theodore Derby, "With that voice, you're going to be a star."

"What are you talking about?" he asked.

"Derby, you sing better than most people who make a living at it."

Said Theodore Derby, "Oh, I couldn't see myself spending all my time singing. I think that would be a rather hollow existence."

"Hollow? Think of the fame, the money, the women . . ."

But Theodore Derby wasn't thinking about any of that. He was flipping through his geometry book and talking about a quiz we had to take that morning.

I would know Theodore Derby, though not well, for the rest of his life. But only after it was over would I even come close to understanding him. In a world where people are admired for living and pursuing a straight line to the top, his was a life of twists and turns that seemingly went nowhere.

In his junior year, he went out for the football team, became the starting quarterback, and led the team to its best record ever. In the spring, as a member of the track team, he set three conference records. At the same time, he was winning a national award for his science project.

But in senior year, Theodore Derby didn't even go out for the football team. The coach, some of the faculty, and most of the students called him a quitter, many to his face. But it didn't seem to bother Theodore Derby. He also didn't run track again, but no one seemed to care much about that.

Instead, Theodore Derby spent the year rebuilding a car in his garage, studying the Thai language, working part-time in a fast food restaurant, and pulling straight As in subjects as diverse as physics and wood shop.

Theodore Derby was a popular fellow. Guys liked to hang out with him. Girls wanted to date him. At some parties he was the center of attention, while at others he would stand along the sidelines and just observe. At one party, he brought along a guitar and played it quite badly. But he had such fun trying that everyone else had fun watching him do it.

He received a dozen scholarships to college but joined the Navy instead. When he got out, he worked his way through college doing a variety of part-time jobs.

After graduating, Theodore Derby started a computer company, made a lot of money, sold the company, and then quietly gave most of the money away. He drove a delivery truck for a few months, went back to school where he got a medic's degree and went to work in a hospital.

He got married, had a couple of kids, stayed home, and took care of them while his wife went to work. Theodore Derby had just established a camp for mentally disabled children when, one evening, he went to bed, had an aneurysm in his sleep, and died.

After the wake, I went out for coffee with Terry Coinston, a guy I knew from high school. Terry, I discovered, was one of Theodore Derby's closest friends.

"Theodore was a nice guy," I said in an obligatory tone, "but he just couldn't stick to anything. He had so much talent in so many ways, he could have really gone somewhere."

"Are you saying the guy was a failure?" asked Coinston with more than a slight edge of annoyance in his voice.

"Well . . . no."

Coinston smiled. "He used to annoy the hell out of me, too, until I realized that he wasn't like you or me or most of the world. He didn't want to 'Go somewhere.' He had no desire to get a degree so he could get a job and then get a promotion and make lots of money so he could buy a bigger house so he could entertain the right people and get another promotion so he could buy a bigger house. Wherever he was at the moment, that's where he wanted to be."

"I know . . ." I tried to interrupt.

Coinston interrupted back. "What motivates most of us meant

nothing to him. He didn't care about money or other people's opinions of him.

"For him, life was a toy box. He'd play with whatever he was doing and when he got bored, he'd go back into the toy box, take out something else, and play with that. Theodore Derby was never going anywhere. He was already there."

I don't know why, but I just wouldn't shut up. "But honestly, what did he ever accomplish?"

"Well," said Coinston, "he was the perfect Theodore Derby."

An ODD View

BECOMING YOUR WIZARD OF ODD:
Be "Theodore Derby."

BEING A WIZARD OF ODD TO OTHERS:
Find the "Theodore Derbys" in your life and tell them how special they are. Tell the people who are not "Theodore Derbys" how special they can be.

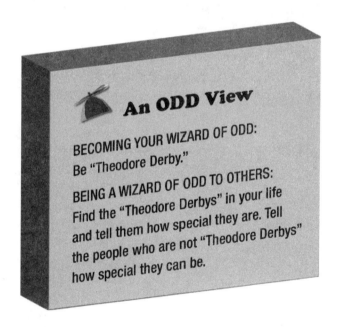

A Kidder

ODDS don't take themselves seriously. Or anyone else.

Because he was a kidder, I often wonder how my grandfather would do in today's politically correct atmosphere. I actually had someone say to me last week, "Oh, I don't like to kid around. I might offend somebody."

Let me clue you in. You're already offending somebody, because you're too tall . . .

. . . you're too short

. . . you're too fat

. . . you're too skinny

. . . you're too black, white, brown, blue . . . you're "too" something.

Walk into a room filled with people and a certain number are just not going to like you. Since you're offending them anyway, you might as well have a good time.

An ODD View

BECOMING YOUR WIZARD OF ODD: Bill Cosby once said that he didn't know the secret for success, but he did know the one for failure: try to please everybody.

BEING A WIZARD OF ODD TO OTHERS: There's a very thick line between having fun and ridicule. Be aware of it.

Labels Are for Bottles, Cartons, and Cans, Not People

Do more than merely accept how ODD you are—embrace it. When you do, you realize that all the Evens you know, beneath the outer shell they present to the world, are just as ODD as you.

There's a lot of talk about discrimination today. It's based on one thought process: *I've met someone like you before so I know who you are.* But the reality is there has never been anyone like you before and there never will be again. Each of us is a once-in-a-universe happening.

But how often do we judge someone by their age, their sex, the color of their skin, the kind of car they drive, where they live, or what they do for a living?

Why do we do that? Easier, that's why. Stick a label on someone, and you don't have to think anymore. But the reality is this: when you meet someone for the first time or the millionth, you always have a choice. You can either learn from them or judge them, but you can't do both. As soon as you choose one, you eliminate the possibility of the other.

We are teachers whether we want to be or not—constantly teaching everyone around us who we are and what we believe life is all about. But we are students only when we choose to be.

This labeling starts quite young in school because teachers are like everyone else; it's easier for them, too. When I was in third grade, my teacher had these various reading groups. You're in one of them because the whole world is in one of them.

The really smart kids were the Cardinals. Then there were the Bluebirds . . . the Robins . . . and my group, the Sparrows. Halfway through the school year, the teacher made up a special reading group just for me . . . the Droppings.

Every day you behaved a certain way because you were treated that way and you were treated that way because you behaved that way and you behaved that way . . .

I remember the very best day I ever had in elementary school. It was in the fourth grade. I went to a Catholic school, but that year we had a lay teacher, Ms. Collins. She put an arithmetic problem on the board and no one could get the right answer. She was calling on all the heavy hitters . . . the Cardinals . . . the Bluebirds . . . they didn't know the answer. Ms. Collins was getting desperate now. She began calling on some Robins. They didn't know the answer either. The Sparrows didn't even know it was an arithmetic problem.

All the time, I was waving my hand like a madman. Every now and then, she'd look over, give me a pathetic sneer, and call on somebody else. After she had called on everybody else, she looked over at me and said, "Well, *Mr.* Powers, what do you think is the correct answer?" Whenever a teacher didn't like you, it was always *Mr.*, even if you were a girl.

I stood up and said, "Well, Ms. Collins, the correct answer is seventeen."

She was astounded. "That's right. The correct answer is seventeen."

But she was hardly about to compliment me. She pointed to me and said to the rest of the class, "Well, if even Mr. Powers can get the right answer . . . if even that guy knows what's going on . . . what's wrong with the rest of you?" and she went on that way for at least ten minutes.

But somewhere during that monologue, she and I became friends. Finally, she looked over at me and said, "John . . ."

". . . Yes, Margaret?"

That was the end of that conversation.

An ODD View

BECOMING YOUR WIZARD OF ODD: Were you a Cardinal, Bluebird, Robin, or Sparrow? Doesn't matter. When you live an ODD life, you become an Eagle and soar to heights where you've never flown before.

BEING A WIZARD OF ODD TO OTHERS: Every time you meet someone, you always have a choice. You can either learn from them or judge them. But you can't do both. When you choose one, you eliminate the possibility of the other. Choose to learn from them.

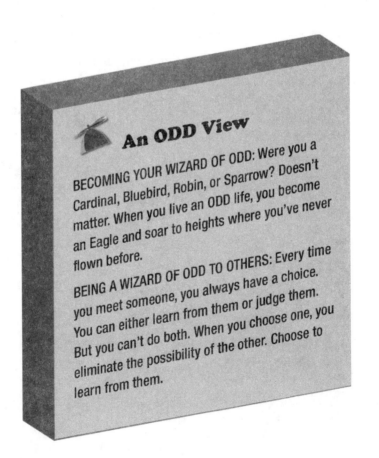

Without Self-Empowerment You Can't Be ODD

To be ODD, you must have power over your own life. If you have no power, then you're Even. People who smother those around them with control discourage them from fully living their lives.

A few years ago, my dad died. He was an easy-going, live-and-let-live kind of guy. He lived a long and good life. Of course, when it's your parent, you always want them to live longer and live better. My dad spent the last few weeks of his life in a nursing home.

One morning, toward the end, I was sitting in his room. I thought he was sleeping. The nurse came in and went to move the box of tissues on the nightstand. All of a sudden, this easy-going, live-and-let-live kind of guy sat up in the bed and quite emphatically said, "Leave that damn box right where it is."

The nurse replied, "Okay," and walked out of the room. I followed her to apologize.

She said, "You don't have to apologize. You have to understand that life is about power. When you're born, the circle of power you possess is about the size of a penny.

"But as you grow up and grow older, that circle gets bigger and bigger and bigger until that moment arrives when . . . you often don't even realize it . . . that circle starts getting smaller and smaller and smaller. Live long enough and you'll reach the point where your dad is. The only thing he can control, in the entire world, is where that box of tissues is on the nightstand.

"The message is clear," she continued. "Learn and teach those around you to live your lives to the outer limits of that circle because it will not be there forever."

She was right. And she was wrong. In terms of physical power, she was right. My dad was down to that one box of tissues on the nightstand. But that's not real power. The real stuff is spiritual. It comes from within.

My dad would often say, "No one can make me happy. No one can make me sad. No one can make me anything unless I first give them the power to do it."

My dad was a person of power until he took his last breath.

Often, we give power over ourselves to people we don't even like. That's what happens every time we let the opinions or actions of someone we dislike upset us.

We even allow strangers to own our emotions. I know I have. A number of years ago, I was carpooling to work with Ronald when another car cut him off. If that had happened to me, I would have gone nuts. You know, the usual: yelling, gestures, pounding on the steering wheel.

Not Ronald. He acted as if he hardly noticed. I asked him how he remained so calm.

Ronald said, "Oh, before, when something like that happened to me, I used to get quite upset. But all it got me was . . . upset. Now, I just tell myself that the other driver must be in a bigger hurry than I am or maybe he didn't see me. Why should I ruin my mood over such a trivial matter? He's not in charge of my attitude. I am."

Do people work *with* you or *for* you? The difference is empowerment. When people are working *with* you, they feel like part of the team and believe they have the power to get the job done in their own, creative way. They are not afraid to make mistakes because they know you will view such choices as part of the learning process. They love who they are and what they do. ODD.

When someone works *for* you, they do what you tell them to. That's it. For the most part, they go through the motions without emotion. They don't feel they have any power, so there is nothing unique, special, or ODD about them at all. Evens.

An ODD View

BECOMING YOUR WIZARD OF ODD: Remind yourself often that self-empowerment is what ODD is all about.

BEING A WIZARD OF ODD TO OTHERS: Empower those around you by encouraging them to truly love who they are and love what they do. That way, you surround yourself with people, not robots; with ODDS, not Evens.

Rules Are the Answers to Yesterday's Questions

What we need are guidelines. What works?

A rule at its highest level of lunacy is called "policy." When someone says, "It's our policy . . ." you now know that whatever she is about to say, it's going to make her life a lot more pleasant than yours.

That's what happens when rules or "policy" win. For example: I leased a car from a major company. I took very good care of it. When the lease terminated, I called the dealer and asked to buy the car. He said, "Certainly. The price is $24,000."

I said, "That's nuts. Even I know the market value of the car is only $15,500."

He replied, "I'm sorry, but it is against policy to negotiate. You see, we gave you such a great leasing deal that we have to make up for it on the back end."

I said, "Well, that would make sense if you were the only person in the world selling cars and I was the only person in the world wanting to buy one."

He responded, "I'm sorry. That's our policy."

So I turned in that car, went somewhere else, and bought another one.

About four months later, I got a phone call from the guy who eventually bought my car. I had forgotten to turn in a set of keys, and he asked me to mail them. I said that I would be glad to, but I would like to know what he had paid for the car. His answer: $15,500.

Don't you think it would have been a lot cheaper for the company I dealt with to simply sell me the car rather than having to clean it up, process all the paperwork, and wholesale it to another company? Policy.

A few years ago, I called a computer company, which is supposedly famous for its attentive customer service, to add to an order I had previously placed. The person who answered the phone said, "You'll have to call back after three PM."

"Why would I do that?"

"Because, according to our records, you are Bob's customer, and he will not be in until after three."

Honest to God.

How many times have you called a company so that you can give them some of your money and you get a recording: "Your call is very important to us"? Like hell it is.

Great companies treat you as unique, special, a one-of-a-kind with needs that are specific to you. They treat you as . . . ODD.

What we need are guidelines that take into consideration the uniqueness of each human being and each situation, that understand and cater to our ODD.

The only policy that makes sense is for a company to make your life so delightful that you dance down the street.

Guidelines, unlike rules or policy, give the person in charge the power to come up with creative solutions. A thinking individual, not a mindless drone, is now making the decision. Personal Power is what being ODD is all about.

Rules tell you what worked yesterday. Guidelines ask you, what will work today?

There are a chosen few who, being naturally clever, instinctively choose guidelines over rules. Fortunately, I am among them. We're called left-handers.

We lefties are far more likely to do what works rather than follow the rules because we know the rules are out to get us.

Look around. If a man's shirt, for instance, has one pocket, it's on the left so a right-hander can, by crossing his body, easily put his pen away. A lefty has to stick his elbow in his neighbor's ear to accomplish the same thing.

Your watch is designed to be worn on the left arm, conveniently out of the way, with the stem toward your hand. Put it on your right arm, where most lefties prefer it, and you have to just about cut off your wrist to change the time.

Our system of writing is designed for right-handers even when you use your left hand because the system goes from left to right. But lefties instinctively go from right to left. That is why so many of us lefties have lousy handwriting. I once had a teacher tell me, "If you ever commit suicide, don't bother leaving a note."

Video cameras are right-eye dominant, but most lefties are left-eye dominant. And don't look now, but virtually every zipper invented is right-handed.

Two examples of rules that have been around for a very long time, but, in today's world, make no sense (we follow them anyway):

The typewriter was invented in the mid-1800s. But the inventor discovered something very quickly. People were typing too fast. They were jamming up his typewriter. This, of course, was a mechanical typewriter. So he redesigned the keyboard so that the left hand would do 60 percent of the typing—not to help out the lefties but to slow down the righties. That is why almost all typing champions are left-handed. We have an innate advantage.

Because of the electric typewriter and the computer, we have not needed that configuration for at least sixty years. About that time, someone designed a new keyboard where, in an eight-hour day, your fingers, instead of traveling eighteen miles, would only travel about a mile and a half. In addition, your typing speed would increase 10 to 25 percent.

Why won't we learn it? Because we have the rule.

Many women have garments that button left-handed. Why? Because when buttons were invented, they were very expensive. Only rich women could afford them. They had other women dressing them. The buttons were right-handed for the dresser, not the woman wearing the garment. The dressers are gone, but the buttons are still left-handed.

No one likes us lefties. Look at our language. "Gauche" is French for left. "Sinister," Latin for left. How about "Left out"? "Leftovers"? "Left-handed compliment"? And my favorite, "He's right."

Rules are about what has been.

Guidelines are about what can be.

ODDs thrive on possibilities.

An ODD View

BECOMING YOUR WIZARD OF ODD:
Love a lefty—especially if you are one.

BEING A WIZARD OF ODD TO OTHERS:
Encourage those around you to solve problems creatively, not by asking, "What are the rules?" but rather, "What will work?"

Win or Lose, Succeed or Fail

One of the ways we stop ourselves from being ODD is by confusing two things that have nothing to do with one another—succeeding and failing and winning and losing.

You are succeeding when you are filling your life with all the feelings, thoughts, and actions that make you unique. You are failing when you stop. That's it. You control all of this.

But winning and losing involve elements of your life that may be beyond your control. When you hold yourself responsible for areas of your life that you cannot control, you just drive yourself nuts. You destroy your self-confidence. You drain your life of ODD.

My mother knew the difference between succeeding and failing and winning and losing.

When I was a kid, my dream was to be a major league baseball player. I had everything it took: desire, discipline, and determination. The only thing I didn't have was talent.

In high school, every year I tried out for the baseball team. All four years, I didn't make it. Coming home from that last tryout, I was so depressed. For the first time, I truly realized that my childhood dream was just that. It would never happen.

I sat down at the kitchen table. Mom was putting dishes away in the cabinets. She tried to say something consoling, but I cut her off.

I said, "Vince Lombardi says, 'Winning isn't everything. It's the only thing.'" For those of you who are not football fans, Vince Lombardi was coach of the first Super Bowl champions, the Green Bay Packers. Actually, that's not what he said, but that's what he's quoted as saying.

Mom sat down next to me at the kitchen table and talked in that tone of voice that said I'd better listen. She began, "Winning isn't anything. You can go an entire lifetime and never win, so it can't be that important. But losing is as much a part of life as breathing. You are going to lose lots of tryouts. Live long enough and you're going to lose jobs . . . and friends . . . and family . . . and dreams.

"Losing and learning to go on and live again is the only kind of winning that truly matters."

The irony is, when you focus on succeeding rather than on winning, you will probably win a lot more often. John Wooden was one of the most successful basketball coaches in history. He talked to his players about many things. He taught them. He coached them. He motivated and inspired them. But he never mentioned winning and losing. Yet they did more winning than any other college team in history.

An ODD View

BECOMING YOUR WIZARD OF ODD: There's nothing wrong with having to start over. There's everything wrong with not starting at all.

BECOMING A WIZARD OF ODD TO OTHERS: When you deal with people, as long as they are doing their best, treat them as the successes they are.

The Last Day Before the First Day

All young children are ODD but then . . .

"Now, Daddy, do I go in the morning or the afternoon?"

Spoken like a true kindergartner. Unfortunately, my daughter is no longer a kindergartner but rather an about-to-be first grader.

"Well, actually, you'll be going in both the morning and the afternoon."

"Uh-huh."

"Hey, first grade is a lot of fun. I've been there. I know."

"Would you like to go back?"

"Well . . . no."

"Uh-huh."

We were sitting on the front porch on a Sunday afternoon, the last day before the first day of first grade. There is a razor chill in the air. A November afternoon has wandered unexpectedly into late August in the Midwest.

Throughout the summer, both my wife and I, as all parents do, have recited the parental praises of first grade. My daughter has listened passively. Even her six-year-old mind seems to realize there are certain situations in life where there are no options and going to first grade clearly seems to be one of them.

When it comes to this school business, my daughter has been around the block a few times. She has been to preschool, and, of course, she is a recent graduate of kindergarten. But she instinctively knows that first grade is an entirely different matter. Now it's time to color inside the lines.

"Can we go to the park?" she asks me. It is her favorite place on earth.

"Right now?"

"Right now."

"Sure."

A few moments later, we are walking across an open field toward the various pieces of playground equipment, which are resting beneath a group of tall trees.

I know the routine. We make cursory visits to the various attractions such as the teeter-totter and the monkey bars. Even the slide does not get much time. Then my daughter heads over to the real destination of her journey, the swings, specifically the one she refers to as the baby swing.

It's the kind that fits all around you. There are regular swings hanging next to it.

She surveys all the swings for a moment as if she is truly debating about which one to choose. This is a recent routine she has developed. She knows that now she's big enough to go on a regular swing and feels a little guilty about not wanting to do that.

"I think I'll go on the baby swing today. Can I do that?"

"You can do whatever you want." I pick her up and plop her into the baby swing.

I don't know how long my daughter would swing before she

got tired of it because she has never asked me to stop. I'm always the one to make the announcement that "It's time to go." When I do, my daughter never whines or complains or begs for more time. You expect a child to do that, but she doesn't.

I always push her from the front so I can look at her face and see her hair fly behind her as she swings up toward the sky.

Sometimes, we talk. She may tell me about her latest trip to the store with Mommy or that, this morning, she called Samantha, her best friend, on her toy phone. Carl, the eight-year-old who lives a few doors down from us, is a popular subject. My daughter is convinced he is out to destroy her. On certain days, she's right.

Sometimes, she and I sing together, her voice "wowing" in and out as she swings past me.

Sometimes, I'll try to tickle her or grab her leg as she goes by on the upswing. She giggles as she defends herself, pushing my hand away or snapping her leg beyond my reach.

But, sometimes, we just enjoy the moment in a serenity of silence, serenaded by the creaking of the chains and the whispering of the swing as it whooshes through the air.

Today is such a day. I try a few questions, but when there is little response, I fall back into my own thoughts and leave her to her own.

She is hanging her head back, looking up through the distant branches of the trees. Perhaps she is dreaming that she has just been launched skyward by the most powerful push in the history of swings. Maybe she sees herself flying up and over the trees, across the park, and past the houses. Now she is even flying over the school, and the higher she flies, the smaller the school gets until it's not even there at all.

After a while, she looks far more relaxed than when we first arrived. A good swing can do that. I gradually slow the swinging down. A sure sign to her that the ride is almost over.

"Time to go home," I say to her.

For the first time in her life she says, "Do we have to?"

"No, we don't."

We swing until the day grows dull with dusk.

Carrying her across the open field: Her arms are thrown around my neck. Her head is resting on my shoulder. I can hear the sleepiness in her voice as she talks to me.

"Even though I'm almost a first grader, can we still come back here and play the way we did today?"

"Of course we can."

"Just you and me?"

"Just you and me."

"And even though I'm almost a first grader, I can still go on the baby swing?"

"Absolutely."

"Any time I want?"

"Any time you want."

The next morning, she walks stoically down the street, her Barbie lunch box gripped tightly in her hand. Her mother and I take turns. One of us holds her hand while the other one circles her with the video camera. When we arrive at the school, our daughter gives us each a hug and kiss. Then she turns and walks down the sidewalk that leads to the main doors of the school. She never looks back. But as she walks through the doors, she holds her lunch box on top of her head and skips down the hall.

The woman next to me says it: "Odd child."

I answer her: "Thank God."

My wife heads to the train station, and I begin the walk back home. Approaching the park, I see a mother standing next to the slide as she places her young child on it. With her hands wrapped around his stomach, she slowly guides him down the slide. The next generation.

I don't have to, but I walk by the baby swing. It is swaying gently in the wind. But it is making a sound I have never heard it make before. I stare at it a few moments and listen, but I can't find the source.

Only when I'm halfway across the field does it occur to me. I'm sure the big ones don't. But I wonder. Do baby swings cry too?

An ODD View

BECOMING YOUR WIZARD OF ODD: Sometimes it's tough being ODD. Okay, a lot of times. But it is always numbing to be Even. You have a choice.

BEING A WIZARD OF ODD TO OTHERS: Teach the students of the world: stay ODD. Don't get Even.

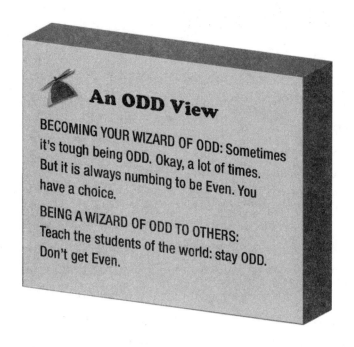

Hope Is the Joy of Planning for, But Not Knowing, the Future

ODDS breathe hope. No hope, you're Even.

An old joke: A guy gets hit by a bus and is stretched out on the street. A cop runs over, takes off his own coat, and gently puts it under the guy's head. The cop asks him, "Are you comfortable?" The guy replies, "Well, I make a living."

Now, you would not have found that joke funny (presuming that you did) if you had heard it before, because you knew what was coming. The fun was in not knowing.

We live in a world of uncertainty. If I ask you what you're doing tomorrow and you tell me, you're guessing. You may not be here tomorrow. I may not be here to check. That's just the way it is.

We all need a certain amount of security—emotional, physical, and financial. But security is like water. You need it to live, but, if that's all you have, you drown.

When you look at the uncertainty of life, you can choose one of two points of view, and your choice will greatly determine just how ODD you are and whether you are adding to or detracting from all the lives you touch.

You can choose stress: "Gee, I don't know what's going to happen, but I know it will be a problem added to all my other problems." Or you can choose hope: "Gee, I don't know what's going to happen, but I am sure it's going to be interesting."

The reality stays the same, but your outlook on life changes dramatically.

Stress strangles the ODD within you. Hope fuels new life into it.

None of us should ever forget that some of the best moments in life are the hope and the excitement of not knowing what's going to happen.

You go to a mystery movie because you don't know the ending. How many relationships have dissolved because each partner became too predictable to the other? You attend a sporting event because you hope your team will win, not because you know it will win. If you absolutely knew what was going to happen at a sporting event, why would you go? Yet, there are Cub fans . . . Who can explain?

In the early 1960s, the New York Yankees were, like today, a great team. But more New Yorkers were going to watch the New York Mets, who were, at that time, the biggest losers in major league baseball. At a Mets game, you never knew what was going to happen.

What could be worse than if you had a book by your bed and every page of that book was a day in your life? When you woke up in the morning, all you had to do was open that book, read the appropriate page, and you'd know exactly what was going to happen that day. What could be worse?

In my presentations, I used to tell my audiences that hope is the second greatest emotion known to the human heart. The first is love. But recently, after my talk, the president of the company before whom I was speaking got up on stage and corrected me.

"Hope," he said, "is the greatest emotion because, if you don't have love, you must have hope in your heart that you will find it."

He's right.

An ODD View

BECOMING YOUR WIZARD OF ODD: Live a life that reflects your belief that "Hope is the joy of planning for, but not knowing, the future."

BEING A WIZARD OF ODD TO OTHERS: Give hope to those around you. Encourage them to plan thoroughly, work hard, give it everything they've got, and then, when they've done everything they can do . . . let go. What happens . . . happens.

William Wilson and the Universe

Everyone we know sees us differently.

Interacting with anyone—a colleague, client, neighbor, friend, even your child—you may see only the sliver of their light that fits into the mosaic of your world. That's the problem.

When dealing with a client, for instance, do you remember that he or she is more than just someone interested in buying your product or services? That person may be a parent, best friend, lover, weekend athlete, musician, poet, sister, brother, daughter, or son. . . . You are just a small part of that person's life, and when you forget that, you miss a wonderful opportunity to nurture your ODD . . . and theirs.

Your ODD feeds off the energy of the ODD in other people—their ideas, interests, experiences, feelings, and points of view. But you cheat yourself out of all of that when you see only the "sliver."

Years ago, when I taught eighth grade, there was a child in my class named William Wilson. I saw just the sliver called the student.

He was a little over five feet tall and weighed twelve pounds, eleven of them dirt. His hair was greasy. His clothes, his shoes . . . everything about him was cruddy.

He rarely came to class, and when he did, he didn't do

anything. Didn't do his homework. Didn't have any friends. He just didn't seem to fit in.

I'm ashamed to admit that, on certain days, I made his life a living hell. When I'd talk to him, one-on-one, he'd shrivel up right in front of me. His head would bow, his shoulders would curl in, he'd look down at his feet, do this nervous little dance, and giggle and whine in a very high-pitched voice.

"Gosh, Mr. Powers, I don't know why I didn't do my homework. I sat there quite a while but nothing happened. I tried and tried and tried . . ."

The sliver I eventually saw was even less than a student. What I saw was a jerk.

One January day, I came out of school long after everyone else had left the building. I got into my car and turned the ignition. I heard nothing. When you live in Chicago, there is no louder sound on a January day than an ignition that makes no sound at all.

Some of you would consider this a minor inconvenience. You're mechanically gifted. I am not. It was a typical Midwestern winter day, eighty-five thousand degrees below zero . . . and a cold front was moving in.

I sat there and tried it and tried it and tried it. Nothing, nothing, nothing.

I got out of the car. I didn't know what to do. Then I saw a figure coming across the parking lot, and it looked like William Wilson. But it couldn't be William Wilson, because this guy was walking tall, the way John Wayne walked down Main Street.

William Wilson came up to me and said, "Having trouble with that car, Mr. Powers?" I noticed that his voice had gotten a lot deeper, too.

"Having trouble with that car?"

When I answered William Wilson, I noticed myself giggling and whining in a high-pitched voice just as he had done in class when he had talked to me.

"Gosh, I don't know why the car won't start. I sat there quite a while but nothing happened. I tried and tried and tried . . ."

William Wilson commanded me, "Get in the car."

So I got in the car. He walked to the front and said, "Pop the hood."

I had no idea how. I began reaching for everything. Finally, I popped the hood.

William Wilson reached under it, fiddled with something for a moment, and then said, "Turn it over."

Of course, when I turned the ignition, the engine just roared up.

William Wilson slammed the hood down, gave it a nice, gentle pat . . . the way John Wayne used to pat that holster.

William Wilson nodded to me and began walking away. Then he thought better of it and came over to the driver's side of the car where I was sitting there looking like the buffoon that I was.

William Wilson said to me, "You know, Mr. Powers, there's a lot more to life than what goes on in your eighth-grade class."

Then he walked across the parking lot . . . into the sunset. That night, he went drinking with my father.

An ODD View

BECOMING YOUR WIZARD OF ODD: Try to see the whole person and not just flickering slivers of light relevant to your life.

BECOMING A WIZARD OF ODD TO OTHERS: When you treat each person as the universe they are, you ignite your ODD as well as theirs.

Another Wizard of ODD

In junior year of high school, I met Mr. Bindel. I had other good teachers before him, but, for whatever reasons, I wasn't ready for them. I was ready for Mr. Bindel. More important, Mr. Bindel was ready for me.

At that point in my life, I considered school the prison sentence I had to serve for the crime of growing up.

Mr. Bindel was the world history teacher, and he was very demanding. In my school, we did not get letter grades. We got straight percentages even on our report cards. Seventy percent was passing. In world history for the first quarter, that's all I wanted to do—pass.

On report-card day, Mr. Bindel walked by my desk and handed me my grades. Slowly, I opened up the report card, found "world history" and raced my finger across to the grade: 96 percent.

I couldn't believe it. My head was spinning. Why, there were quarters when you could have added up all my grades, and I wouldn't have gotten 96.

I knew luck had played a role here somewhere. I must have guessed right on every one of those multiple-choice questions. But unless you have been there, unless you have spent a lot of time at the bottom of the heap, you don't know how I felt.

Every school day, for ten years, I had gone somewhere where I was expected to fail. Every school day, I succeeded at fulfilling everyone's expectation of me.

But that day, in Mr. Bindel's class, for the first time I felt good about something that had happened in school. I felt proud. I felt taller. For the first time, on report-card day, I didn't take the long way home . . . through Guam.

I liked that feeling of success, and I made up my mind that, one way or the other, I was going to keep that 96 percent.

Second quarter, 94 percent. Third quarter, 97 percent, and the fourth-quarter final grade that I received in world history was 98 percent.

On the last day of school, when Mr. Bindel had handed out the grades, he said, "Mr. Powers, I'd like to see you after class."

Students like me have a certain strategy. When you absolutely have to talk to a teacher, what you do is you talk long enough so that by the time you've finished, that teacher has died of natural causes.

So I walked up to him. "Hi, Mr. Bindel. Boy, Mr. Bindel, I bet you're really surprised by the grades I got this year, huh, Mr. Bindel? I bet that first quarter really surprised you, huh, Mr. Bindel . . . and by the way, how do you think the Cubs are going to do this year? They're kind of weak in the outfield and they could use some hitting . . ."

Mr. Bindel said, "Shut up."

So I did.

"Actually," said Mr. Bindel, "the only quarter that did not surprise me was the first quarter when you got ninety-six percent because it was a mistake. You were supposed to get sixty-nine percent, but I inadvertently reversed the numbers putting them into the report card.

"I didn't catch the mistake until we were three weeks into the next quarter. By then, I had noticed a change in you. You were . . . paying attention. You were asking questions other than 'May I go to the washroom?' In other words, you acted like you deserved that ninety-six percent, so I just thought I'd let it go and see what happened.

"The point is, Mr. Powers, like virtually every student in this school who isn't getting out of it what he should, you could do virtually anything you wanted to do the moment you believe you can do it."

The moment you believe.

❋

How old would you be if you didn't know how old you are? How tall would you be if you didn't know how tall you are? How smart would you be if you didn't know how smart you are? In other words, how ODD would you be if you let yourself simply "Be"?

❋

I call Mr. Bindel my wizard because a wizard gives you what you've already got, but you'd never have it unless the wizard gave it to you first. Doesn't make sense. That's why they're called wizards. All great teachers, whether they are standing in front of a classroom, living their careers, at home raising their children, lying in a hospital bed, or driving a city bus—every great teacher is a wizard to the children in his or her life, giving them faith in themselves.

An ODD View

BECOMING YOUR WIZARD OF ODD: Look for the wizards in your life. They will help you discover your own Wizard of ODD.

BEING A WIZARD OF ODD TO OTHERS: A great wizard gives others faith in themselves. That's what makes them wizards.

Diversity (Don't Marry Your Cousin)

Of course, if your cousin is really cute . . .

A group of biologists asked a simple question, "What role does sex play in nature?" If your response is, "Duh . . . for reproduction," you are wrong. There are certain species that have only females, who reproduce on their own.

It just so happens that a mountain range in New Mexico provided a natural laboratory that could help these biologists answer this question. In two small ponds of water, separated by only a couple of hundred miles, lived a tiny species of fish. There was a major difference.

One pond contained both male and female of these fish, while the other one had only females of this species, which reproduced autonomously.

After studying a few generations of these fish, the biologists discovered some interesting facts. The fish with two parents were far stronger than the females-only in fighting off the viruses and bacteria, which were their major enemies. The biologists determined that this was because the two-parent fish were created from a more diverse genetic pool. The biologists further concluded that any species that reproduced exclusively with females was in its final stages of evolution before extinction.

We human beings have instinctively realized the advantages of a diverse genetic pool for a long time. "Don't marry your cousin" is based on this theory. In addition, many African tribes have customs that encourage their young people to seek mates outside of the immediate area.

Diversity works in all aspects of our lives. A weight trainer told me, "You cannot keep doing the same exercises because your muscles 'catch on,' and they adjust rather than get stronger. You must continually vary your exercises. Diversify them."

Most financial advisors believe you should diversify your investments.

Great thinkers diversify their thoughts. They are constantly looking for new ideas, meeting new people, and doing new things.

ODDs learn that diversity leads to great achievements.

An ODD View

BECOMING YOUR WIZARD OF ODD: Realize that strength through diversity is a natural process and not just a politically correct one.

BEING A WIZARD OF ODD TO OTHERS: Help others to achieve a diversity of ideas.

The ODD Lady in Aisle Nine

Too much of a coincidence—meeting a super lady at a supermarket. But it happened anyway.

When my first book came out in paperback, my agent at that time suggested I have an autographing session, not in a bookstore, but in a supermarket. He said, "There are a lot more people in a supermarket. What have you got to lose?"

Only my dignity. I was scheduled to be there for ninety minutes, and, for the first eighty-eight, not one person stopped at my table. Most of them looked at me as if I were in a bookstore trying to sell them a can of peas.

Then I saw her: an overweight, sloppily dressed woman, a little boy hanging onto her hand, walking down the aisle straight toward me. I thought, *Oh, great. She's going to walk by me, eat the frozen food section, and then have all the cake and ice cream in the store for dessert.*

But they didn't walk by me. She and the little boy stopped and stood in front of my table. He stared at me, his eyes growing wide, as he listened to her words.

She said, "You see this man sitting here? A thousand years from now, almost nothing will have survived from our civilization. Oh, perhaps pieces of some buildings. A few paintings. But the stories of our world, our lives, the dreams, the disasters, the wars, and the wisdom will all be preserved in words written by people like him. He is a writer. He is an artist."

I asked the little boy for his name and signed the book to him. Then he and this quietly elegant lady walked away.

If ignorance was fat, she was a size three and I would not have been able to get down the aisle. But she also reminded me of something else that we, too often, forget: all of us are artists.

✻

A few years ago, I was sitting on my front porch writing a book. At the same time, a local carpenter was rebuilding one end of the porch. We took our lunch break at the same time. As we sat on the steps eating our sandwiches, he said to me, "I just can't imagine someone sitting down and writing a book. That is beyond my comprehension."

I replied, "You know, at this very moment, I was thinking that if someone asked me to rebuild a porch, I would not know where to begin. It is beyond my comprehension."

I don't know what you do, but if you do it really well, you are an artist. Like all artists, your work is unique. Like all artists, your work can have universal appeal. Like all artists, your impact on future generations is immeasurable. You enrich the lives of one generation so it can nurture the next.

Like all artists, you are ODD.

An ODD View

BECOMING YOUR WIZARD OF ODD:
Remember, ODDs don't let their "outside" define their "inside."

BEING A WIZARD OF ODD TO OTHERS:
ODDs know that great teachers are everywhere, even in supermarket aisles. Find them. Learn from them. Become one of them.

Never Confuse Talent with Character

Last night, I watched a television interview of a major league star. He was introduced as a great guy. He's not. In fact, he's an incredibly self-centered jerk. To put it another way, that major league star is no Calvin Cutnose.

A number of years ago, I coached a Little League team. The star was Chris Adams. The most enthusiastic and by far the worst player on the team was Calvin Cutnose. Everyone played better than Calvin. No one enjoyed it more.

Calvin was a bouncer. He spent more than his share of time on the bench, and, when he sat there, he bounced. When he ran out on the field and when he ran in, he'd bounce. No matter what position he played, he'd be bouncing. He even bounced a little in the batter's box.

His mother told me that baseball was Calvin's all-consuming passion. He loved playing it, watching it, listening to it, reading about it, and talking about it.

I identified with Calvin Cutnose. When I was a kid, I was passionate about baseball, too. I had even less talent than Calvin.

Calvin Cutnose had severe allergies, so he'd occasionally miss a game. I noticed that when Calvin wasn't there, the team never played very well. I believe his enthusiasm was contagious, and it seemed to push the other players to do better. I doubt they were even aware of Calvin's effect.

One Saturday afternoon, we had a game scheduled at three o'clock. A heavy rain, which had been falling all day, turned to drizzle around two-thirty. Regardless, I got out of my easy chair, went into the garage, which was flooded, got into my car and drove over to the field's parking lot, which was also flooded. Most of the infield was under water. A lone person sat in the stands. I walked over to him and said, "Calvin, there is no game."

That team finished the season by winning the championship game. Chris Adams, the star, hit two home runs. But the heart and soul of that team was Calvin Cutnose.

An ODD View

BECOMING YOUR WIZARD OF ODD: Remember that you do not have to be the best at what you do. But if it's truly what you want to do, if it is part of what makes you ODD, you are always the best you can be.

BEING A WIZARD OF ODD TO OTHERS: A great team is one where the whole is greater than the pieces. Be sure you have a Calvin Cutnose, because people like him are the glue that holds the pieces together.

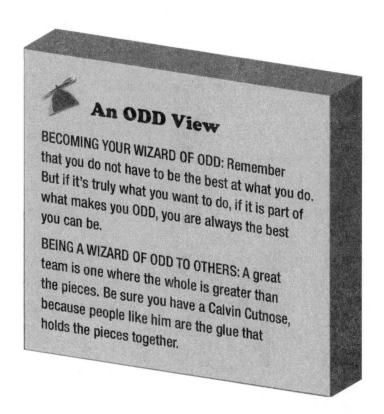

The Older You Get, the Wiser You Get

I once asked my grandfather, only half-kidding, how he got to be so smart. He replied, "When you live as long as I have, you get a lot more time to learn. You can use all that experience to widen your horizon or narrow it. The choice is yours."

Did you know that the average sixty-five-year-old knows four times more than the average college graduate?

When I was in my twenties, I was writing an article that required me to interview a number of people who were in their sixties. Quite often, the interviewee would mention someone or something in such a way that he presumed I knew what he was talking about. When I admitted my ignorance, he would be shocked. "How can you not know that?"

Simple. I wasn't alive at the time. For him, it was part of his life experience. For me it was . . . well . . . history I had yet to learn.

Being a lot older now, when I talk to young people, I find myself on the opposite side of that conversation.

We are a nation that, for the most part, is obsessed with youth for three reasons:

First of all, network television, in particular, focuses on young people because, as far as it is concerned, that's where the money is. Television is an advertising medium. Programs are presented only because the industry knows we will not watch the commercials without them. Television aims its programming at the young for a very good reason—commercials influence young people far more successfully than they do older people.

It is well known that television seeks viewers who are, primarily, between ages eighteen and thirty-five. If you are beyond that age, when you watch prime-time television, listen carefully. The vast majority of programs are telling you to get lost.

This is ironic, since people with the most disposable income are over sixty-five. But instead of relying on commercials, older people depend on both their personal experiences and the experiences of those around them in making choices about what to buy. To put it succinctly, older people, at least most of them, are wiser.

Second, we are living in an age of exploding information. According to one study, all the information in the world is doubling every eighteen months. The ones who know the most about the newest information are the people who are learning it at the moment—usually young people. In addition, with young people, the new information is writing on a clean slate. Young people don't have to discard old ideas when learning the new ones.

Third, we are a nation of immigrants who worship the concept of new beginnings, fresh starts, and cheering for the underdog. All of this translates into "young." One of the hottest words in our language today is "change." The concept of "tradition" is considered dumb and the exact opposite of change. We identify tradition with the old and change with the young.

Our culture reflects this bias against age. Those who are "politically correct" have no problems telling jokes about old people. Being a consumer nation, "new" is always better than "old." Although it is now becoming more common to preserve older buildings, the first instinct of most communities is still to tear them down and replace them with new ones.

Many parts of our society still encourage people to retire at sixty-five. But the vast majority of us no longer do physical work, so there's really no need to stop working at that age except for the fact that we're now defined as "old."

It's great if you want to stop working at sixty-five. But what if you don't? Should you still be forced to because you're "old"? My uncle was a highly successful salesman, but his company had a strict policy of retiring people at sixty-five. He was so depressed about losing his job that he went home, sat in the front window, and waited for death to come. He wasn't disappointed.

The biggest source of untapped wisdom in this country is our old people. In small ways, we are catching on. Just recently, we realized the generation that fought World War II is dying out and this is our last chance to hear their wisdom. A number of best-sellers have been based on their words.

There are even a few companies and their customers who are learning to appreciate the value of older employees. I walked into a discount store with Claire, a friend of mine. Two years earlier, Claire had managed such a store. We had a question about a particular product. We also had a choice of going to the counter of a teenager or an "old" person.

I started toward the teenager. Claire stopped me. "Let's see . . ." she said. "The teenager is probably thinking about the homework he still has to do, how far he's going to get with his girlfriend on their next date, the pimple that's growing on his forehead . . . I suspect the old guy is thinking about his job."

For the most part, in most organizations, older men and women are considered inflexible, living in the past, and just plain stupid.

Yell a message loud enough and long enough, and people will begin to believe it. Individuals seem to lose confidence in themselves as they grow older simply because society sends subtle (and not so subtle) messages that they are becoming antiquated. Yet, some of the most successful people in our history have been older and old. Two examples from the food industry are Ray Kroc, who started his McDonalds at the age of fifty-four, and Colonel Sanders, who began building his Kentucky Fried Chicken empire at the age of sixty-five.

It's difficult for young people to comprehend being old. After all, if you're twenty-four, that's as old as you've ever been. Young people don't realize that being old is just a phase one goes through, which is also true of being young.

An old joke about an old lady who, with her grandson, was watching an antique-car parade: She said, "I had a good time in the backseat of every one of them."

Interesting. Many older people try to maintain some of the positive aspects of being young, such as staying in good physical shape. But few young people seek out the advantages of being older, such as encouraging older people to share their wisdom with them.

In a recent conversation, I said to an elderly lady, "You're ninety-three years old and you live in a three-story house?"

She corrected me. "I'm ninety-three years old *because* I live in a three-story house."

A great thing about being old is that there are so many people inside of you. If you're . . . say . . . sixty-five, you have a ten-year-old inside, a twenty-year-old, a thirty-year-old, a forty-year-old . . . and so on. The younger you are, the fewer the lives you've led.

To grow wiser as you grow older seems to be a natural process. To be young and stupid is to be expected. To be old and stupid is pathetic. With each passing day, if all goes well, you become wiser and just a bit more ODD.

An ODD View

BECOMING YOUR WIZARD OF ODD: Remind yourself, "I'm wiser today than I was yesterday. I will be wiser tomorrow."

BEING A WIZARD OF ODD TO OTHERS: Surround yourself with people of all ages. Remember, each person is a book waiting to be read. Some of the best books ever written were created thousands of years ago . . . or will be published tomorrow.

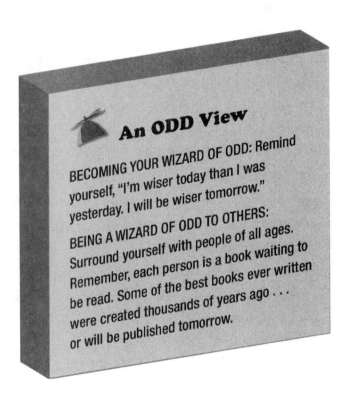

An ODD View

She has picked me up from the airport and is now driving me to my presentation. She's an older lady, probably in her late sixties. Handing me a brochure, she begins telling me about her group. But I'm not listening. I've been distracted by the photo of a young, attractive woman on the front of the brochure. The caption under the photo identifies her as the president of the organization. But I thought the woman driving me was the president. . . .

My driver notices my confusion. "Yes, that's me," she says. "A very old picture of a very young me. I was out of town when my club needed a photo. They called the house and talked to my husband and that was what he sent them.

"A few weeks later, when I returned back home and saw the brochure, I just about had a stroke. I mean, that brochure had been sent to virtually every woman I know in this town, and I could imagine every single one of them snickering at that picture, making comments such as, 'Does she really believe she still looks like that?' and 'Who does she think she's kidding?' I don't think I've ever been so angry.

"My husband was at home working in his office. I barged into his office waving that brochure and began screaming at him. 'How could you do this to me? Sending in a forty-year-old picture. Do you know how embarrassed I am? How could you be so insensitive?'

"Then, without warning, all of the anger drained out of me. After all, there was nothing I could do. The brochures had already been mailed. I put my hands over my face and just wept.

"That upset my husband. I'm not a crier. In all the years I've known him, he hasn't seen me cry more than two or three times.

He tried to say something, changed his mind, and began again.

"'What's going on here?' he asked me.

"I looked up and gave him a cold-stone stare. Holding up the brochure so he could clearly see the photo, I asked him, 'Did you or did you not send in this picture?'

"'You know I did. . . .'

"'What were you thinking?' I was yelling again. But, for the first time, I noticed his puzzled expression.

"'They asked me to send in a photo of you so I did.'

"'Not one that was forty years old.' I pointed to the picture in the brochure. 'Do I look like that?'

"'To me, you do.'

"I know my husband. I could tell he wasn't kidding. I suddenly realized . . . in his eyes, I wasn't just this old lady who only wore sensible shoes. I was still the young, beautiful woman he had fallen in love with so many years ago. For the second time in less than two minutes, I cried again."

An ODD View

BECOMING YOUR WIZARD OF ODD: When you are ODD, you see what you know is there. When you are Even, you see what you are told is there.

BEING A WIZARD OF ODD TO OTHERS: Joyously share your ODD views with those around you. But don't be surprised if they don't see them.

Listen to the Fool

Most people consider fools to be individuals who are beyond redemption. Most people are wrong.

In every little world—at the office, in an organization, or in a community—there's a fool. Look around. If you can't find the fool . . . it's you.

Fools are out of the mainstream. They seem to enjoy annoying everyone around them. They see life differently than the rest of us do. Listening to a fool will often get you to look into corners of your mind that you have never searched before.

Therein lies their value.

A popular expression today is "Think outside the box." Fools live outside the box. Fools are ODD. Very.

They look at things from a very different, coldly logical perspective. That's why we think they're fools.

A few examples:

A major eastern university built a new library. At the opening-night reception, an employee of the university, a well-known fool, said to the architect, "I am so excited to meet you. I just cannot fathom all the talents you must possess to build a library—designing the building, figuring out the traffic flow, determining the weight of the books so you can build sufficiently strong shelves . . ."

The architect had forgotten about that last one. The opening of the library had to be postponed eighteen months.

A number of years ago, I had written a stage play. In the second act, there was a long, dramatic scene followed by two jokes. The first joke was getting a bigger laugh than the second one. That's not the way it should be. The second joke should always get the bigger laugh. So I flipped them. Didn't matter. The joke now in the first position still got the bigger laugh. So I wrote two new jokes. That didn't help either.

At that time, one of the guys in the show was, in my opinion, a fool. Six weeks into the run, during a rehearsal, I was again rewriting these two jokes when this actor came over to me and said, "Do you want to know what your problem is here?"

"Yes," I said with all the sarcasm I could shove into that one word. "Enlighten me."

He said, "I'd be delighted to. There is a fourteen-minute dramatic scene, which has built up a lot of emotional pressure within the audience. They want to relieve that tension, which is what laughter does. They are looking for a reason to laugh, and your first joke is their opportunity. That is why the second joke will never top the first one. In fact, the laughs you get with both jokes have little to do with what you've written. It's the location of the moment, not the content. The audience wants to laugh at that point, and they are going to, one way or the other."

He was right. Being a writer, an "expert" with words, I presumed that the key to my problem was to be found in words rather than in understanding the overall energy flow of the play.

One night, just to test out the fool's theory, I wrote gibberish for that moment. It still got a solid laugh.

There's an old saying, "If two people are thinking alike, you don't need one of them."

But you can always use a fool.

Virtually every hugely successful inventor, artist, business person, historical figure, or philosophical thinker was, at one point, considered by the vast majority of people to be a fool.

What do you call a successful fool? A genius.

An ODD View

BECOMING YOUR WIZARD OF ODD:
Listen to the fool, especially the one within you. After all, all fools are ODD.

BEING A WIZARD OF ODD TO OTHERS:
Today, teamwork is an important part of any organization. When you utilize the fool's unique outlook, you realize that one does not have to be a "team player" to make valuable contributions to the team.

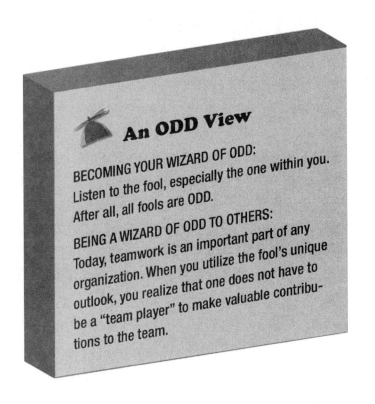

The Jimmy Flaskin Rule

Growing up on Chicago's South Side, there were a million kids in my neighborhood. Jimmy Flaskin was one of them. Although he was popular, his quiet demeanor bordered on sullen.

If a big guy picked on an easy target, Jimmy Flaskin would step in and defend him. This was simply not done. Jimmy Flaskin did it anyway. He wasn't the toughest kid in the neighborhood. But everybody knew one thing about Jimmy Flaskin: he never backed down from anybody. Ever. He didn't win every fight. But then, he never clearly lost one either.

Eventually, the bullies of the neighborhood got the message. If Jimmy Flaskin was around, don't pick on one of the lambs. It just wasn't worth the effort.

In sophomore year of high school, Jimmy Flaskin was in my math class. The teacher was an idiot. For the first eight months, we learned nothing. Finally, the administration caught on, fired the guy, and brought in a good teacher, Mr. Kabal. But even he knew he couldn't teach an entire year of math in the few remaining weeks of the school year.

On the day of the final exam, Mr. Kabal came up with his own solution. After handing out the test, he announced to the class, "People, I'm going out for a cup of coffee . . . perhaps to Brazil. Good luck!" and he walked out the door.

Even we could figure out what was going on, and we immediately began an orgy of cheating: yelling out answers, switching papers, taking out the book. . . . As I was busily cheating with the others, I glanced over at Jimmy Flaskin to see what he was doing. He was looking down at his desk taking his math test.

As we walked back home through the neighborhood, a bunch of us were doing the usual after-test chattering. "What did you put down for number fifteen?" "Was seven the right answer for number twenty-eight?" That sort of stuff. I kept waiting for Jimmy Flaskin to call us a bunch of dirty, rotten cheaters, because, indeed, we were. He said nothing.

Now the stakes were high. Fail this test, and it was six weeks of summer school. Not only did that take a big bite out of your summer, but it was also socially humiliating. At that time, no one went to school during the summer voluntarily simply to get some course work out of the way. Only flunkies went, and the entire neighborhood knew because, every morning, they would see you leave your house on the way to summer school.

A few days later, we were back in math class to receive our final grade. Only one person failed. Only one had to go to summer school. Jimmy Flaskin. The rest of the class didn't think it was because he was honest. They just presumed he was so stupid he couldn't even cheat his way through. As far as I know, Jimmy Flaskin never said anything to anyone about it.

As I said, I grew up in a neighborhood with a million kids. I can hardly recall any of them. But I remember Jimmy Flaskin.

An ODD View

BECOMING YOUR WIZARD OF ODD:
The Jimmy Flaskin rule: Do what's right because it's right. That's all there is to this rule.

BEING A WIZARD OF ODD TO OTHERS:
You can't teach the Jimmy Flaskin rule to others. You can only live it yourself. Eventually, those around you will catch on. Well, some of them will.

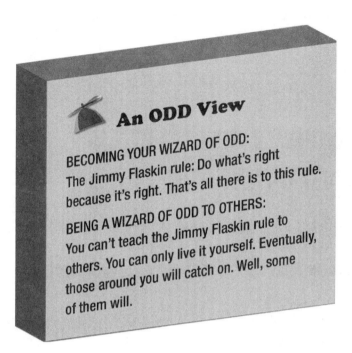

Are You Busy Wasting Time?

Evens like to "get ready . . . get set . . ." endlessly. It is the ODDs who "go." Evens busy themselves with the means, while ODDs focus on attaining the ends.

Evens love to wallow in busy work because it gives them the delusion they are getting things done. They are plodders, often losing sight altogether of their goals. Evens "put in" their time.

ODDs are achievers. They get things done.

Committees, at least the bad ones, can be great for focusing on what doesn't matter. They spend a ton of time on the means while forgetting about the end.

I sat on a nonprofit committee for three months, which met once a week. Their stated purpose was to raise money for youth programs. Compared to them, molasses moves at the speed of light. They loved telling one another, "Define your terms."

If a fire had broken out in a corner of that room, by the time we defined "smoke," we would have all been ashes.

The problem with that committee was that merely being at the meeting became more important than the problem solving that was supposed to be occurring at the meeting. No one got any credit and no one got any blame, so no one got anything done.

When it comes to minor matters, plodders often seek perfection. That way, you can put in more time. When I was a college student, I worked a summer at a freight-car company. Like most lousy employees, I was a plodder. I was an Even.

One morning, my job was to paint over the rust spots on a series of old freight cars. I was standing there carefully dabbing out the various spots of rust. The foreman came by and observed me for a moment. Then he walked up, grabbed my paint bucket, shoved me out of the way, took a few steps back, and splashed the entire gallon of paint onto the side of the freight car. Handing me the empty bucket, he said, "Spread it around and get your ass moving to another job. This ain't the *Mona Lisa,* kid."

Now, when I'm doing something and I realize that it doesn't deserve the time I'm giving it, I remind myself, "It ain't the *Mona Lisa*. Just get it done."

❊

Mark was a salesman whose job required a certain amount of schmoozing with his clients—taking them to dinner, golf outings, that sort of thing. He became a great schmoozer. But in the process, he forgot that the purpose of schmoozing was to sell more product. He almost lost his job before he realized that he had to focus on the passion that had brought him to the job to begin with—selling. He was getting ready, getting set, but not going. He wasn't selling.

Every college has a number of "get ready, get set, but *never go*" students. They often change majors and schools and manage to accumulate hundreds of college credits without ever earning a degree. These students hang around a college for the same reason some people hang around bars. It is a comfortable environment.

Such students have focused completely on the process and have forgotten their goal of getting a degree.

Why have so many of us allowed ourselves to get ready, get set . . . but not *go*? Fear.

When you decide to live a life that relishes your ODD, change is going to occur. You're gambling the change is going to make your life better, not worse, and that's scary. The unknown always is.

If you are thinking Even, maybe you're scared because you perceive that the stakes are too high. At such times, it's good to remember that although many things in life are important, none of them are serious. No matter what you do, no matter how great, silly, or stupid, it is virtually certain that, in a very short amount of time, no one is going to know, care, or remember.

That would be just as true if you were the ruler of the world. In just a hundred years, in terms of the universe hardly the blink of an eye—you and I and everyone else alive today, at least physically, will be the dust on someone's furniture.

An ODD View

BECOMING YOUR WIZARD OF ODD: Be dust that had fun. Focus on the goal, not the process.

BECOMING A WIZARD OF ODD TO OTHERS: Remind those around you about that old saying in basketball: "You miss all the shots you never take."

How Badly Do You Want It?

Evens quit. ODDs persist.

ODDs often ask themselves the same question: "How badly do I want it?"

Well, how badly do you want it?

The problem is that the vast majority of us, the vast majority of the time, are quitters. We give up on diets, relationships, jobs, school . . . and being ODD.

I was talking to a CEO. He asked me what I did for a living. I told him I was a professional speaker and that the next day I would be presenting a program called, "The Five Disciplines of Powerful People: How to Keep the Promises You Make to Yourself."

He said, "I hope they don't listen to you."

"Why?" I asked him.

"Because," he replied, "I'm the vice-president of a major health-club chain. We have facilities in virtually every state in the nation, and our club is not a cheap one to join. Our studies reveal that for every one hundred people who do join, eighty use our facilities once or never. Nineteen use them two to four times and then never again. Only one out of a hundred people actually follows through and becomes a regular user of our club. If the number just went to two out of a hundred, that means we would have to double our facilities. We'd go out of business. Thank God the vast majority of people are quitters."

You know that's true. Walk into a health club in January and it's packed with people trying to keep their New Year's resolutions. Go back in March and the place is basically empty.

Approximately 40 percent of the people who begin college never graduate. On the doctoral level, 90 percent of the candidates do all the course work, pass the qualifying exam, and . . . never complete their dissertations. Ninety percent can't finish what they started.

Why do companies offer "money back guarantees"? They know that even if you are unhappy with the product, you will most likely not bother to follow through by returning the product and asking for your money back.

Think about it. The concept of rebates is ridiculous. "Buy my product for one hundred dollars, fill out this form, mail it to me, and I'll send you back twenty dollars." Common sense dictates that the seller simply charge eighty dollars for the product to begin with.

Ah, but the seller knows that the vast majority of people do not have the persistence to follow through and send in the form. Often, only in the mind of the buyer at the time of purchase has twenty dollars been saved.

In order to be physically strong, you have to lift heavy things all the time. Why would developing spiritual muscles be any different? ODDs persistently "lift" and conquer spiritual challenges.

The most successful individuals are not necessarily the smartest, most talented or luckiest. But they are the most persistent. Read the biographies of famous people and you will see that they "fail" far more often than the rest of us. They don't consider such moments failures but rather merely obstacles to be overcome in pursuit of their dreams.

Growing up, we actually have to learn the concept of failure from the adults around us. When an infant is learning to walk, he or she repeatedly falls down. But rather than consider it failure, they instinctively realize it is simply a part of the learning process. If infants understood the concept of failure, most of us would still be crawling around today.

As long as you are striving toward who you truly are, you are successful. When you stop, you are not.

Jim Valvano was a college basketball coach who won a national championship. A few years later, he was diagnosed with terminal cancer. His battle cry against this enemy was "Never, never ever quit." He lost his life, but he never failed. Jim Valvano succeeded in totally living every day true to who he was. ODD.

An ODD View

BECOMING YOUR WIZARD OF ODD: The most successful individuals are not the smartest, most talented, or luckiest, but they are the most persistent.

BEING A WIZARD OF ODD TO OTHERS: Lead by example. You do not have to tell people to follow you. They will do so with incredible loyalty once they realize you are persistently giving every ounce of energy to pursuing the promise you all share.

ODDs Demand Excellence

Rewarding mediocrity will turn you from ODD to Even.

In college, I took a course from Dr. Allis, who was a good teacher. Not brilliant but good. He gave a midterm exam, which had four sections. Each section received a numerical grade. Dr. Allis would then add the four numbers to determine the letter grade of each student.

When I received my midterm test back, I discovered that I had missed an A by a point. But Dr. Allis had added the four sections of my test incorrectly by a point. That one point was costing me an A.

After the test, I went up to Dr. Allis and showed him my test paper and the miscalculation he had made.

He explained, "I have a strict policy about not changing grades."

I said, "But Dr. Allis, you don't understand. You added the numbers incorrectly."

He replied emphatically, "No, you don't understand. I do not change grades under any circumstances. Besides, this is only the midterm. It's not your final grade."

Of course, after getting my final exam back, I discovered that I had missed an A for the course by just one point—the point I had lost when Dr. Allis had mistakenly added my midterm scores.

After class that day, I went up and had the same conversation with Dr. Allis that I had had with him after the midterm. He adamantly refused to give me the point I had earned so I would get an A for the course.

"Okay, okay," I said to him. "Why don't we take a step back here? Let's just say that this one point was not the difference between my getting an A or a B but rather it was the difference between my getting a D or an F? In other words, if I did not get this point, I would fail the course. Then would you give it to me?"

Dr. Allis thought about that a moment. "Well, in all honesty, I would."

I said, "I see. You don't mind mediocrity. It's excellence you're against."

I got a B.

❊

I was a teacher myself. I taught my students to strive for excellence. Or so I thought.

One afternoon, I got caught doing what I condemn. I walked into a class to give an examination. The class virtually begged me to postpone the test for a week, so I did.

Afterward, one of my best students came up to me and asked, "You know what you did today?"

"Yes, I postponed a test."

"Well," he replied, "you did that, too. But, more important, what you also did was reward every person in that room who didn't study for your test while punishing those of us who did. Next week, I'll have to study all over again. You rewarded the mediocre and punished the excellent."

I replied, "You should have said something."

He said, "What? And be hated by almost everyone else in the class? It was your job to hold the line, not mine."

He was right. That was the last test I postponed.

❊

When my daughter was in the first grade, each child had to begin the school year with a box of crayons. If a child could not afford it, the school would provide one. Six weeks into the school year, one little boy had chewed on, broken, and basically destroyed his box of crayons.

The teacher did not lecture the boy or in any other way call attention to his actions. She immediately told all the other children in his group to share with him, which, of course, they did.

I went to the school and complained.

"Sharing is good," said the teacher.

I replied, "So is accountability. And sharing is only good if you choose to share. What lesson did the boy learn? That not taking care of his crayons has no consequences? What lesson did the other children, including my daughter, learn? That even if you take care of your property, you may be forced to give some of it to people who didn't?"

The same is true in the business world. If you reward mediocrity, then you will get more of it. I was walking down the street with my cousin, Leon, an ODD fellow. I began to walk into a mini-mart to buy a pack of gum. Leon stopped me. He said, "Buy it across the street. It's a nickel cheaper."

I said, "A nickel! That's not worth crossing the street."

Leon replied, "You don't understand. Every time you spend your money, you are voting. You're saying to the recipient, 'You are doing a better job than your competitor, so I'm voting for you.' If you buy your gum here, you are saying to the fellow across the street, 'I don't care that you're striving to be excellent at your job, I'm voting for the other guy anyway.' You are undermining excellence as well as our entire capitalistic system all for a lousy nickel."

I bought my gum across the street.

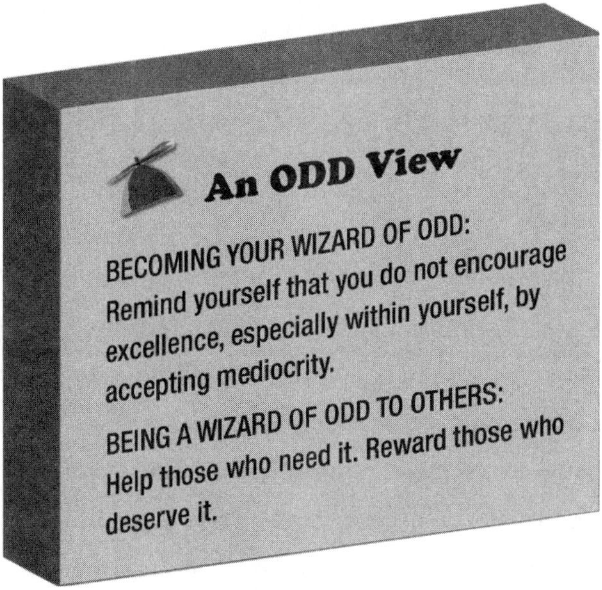
An ODD View
BECOMING YOUR WIZARD OF ODD:
Remind yourself that you do not encourage excellence, especially within yourself, by accepting mediocrity.
BEING A WIZARD OF ODD TO OTHERS:
Help those who need it. Reward those who deserve it.

You'll Never See Your ODD in the Rearview Mirror

If you spend all your time looking in the rearview mirror at where you've been, you will never discover just how ODD you are.

You listen to someone constantly telling you there is no way you are going to achieve your dreams because you've never achieved them before. That voice will not shut up, and, after a point, you become totally convinced it's right. That voice is yours.

Too many of us talk to ourselves all day, making negative, whining, and disparaging comments that we would never say to our friends. We practice emotional cannibalism, allowing our negative thoughts to devour our spirits.

You'll hear somebody say something like, "I'm not very good at math." What that person should be saying is, "Up to this point in my life, I have not been good at math."

Martha, my neighbor, was trying to quit smoking. One morning, I asked her how she was doing.

"Oh, not very well," she replied. "I got down to ten cigarettes a day, but I just couldn't quit. My friends were giving me a hard time. My husband was teasing me. I gave up. I have tried so often to give up cigarettes. I guess I just can't do it."

I asked her how many cigarettes she had been smoking a day before she tried to quit.

"About two packs."

That's forty cigarettes. In other words, Martha went from smoking forty cigarettes a day to ten, a success rate of 75 percent, but she still defined herself as a failure. That's what Martha saw when she looked in her rearview mirror—someone who repeatedly had tried to quit smoking but had always "failed."

I suggested to Martha that she buy her usual two packs of cigarettes that day, take the ones she could live without, and put them in the middle of her kitchen table. She should do that every day. That way, she could literally see her success: all the cigarettes she had chosen not to smoke. In other words, instead of looking in her rearview mirror, where she had a long history of not being able to quit smoking, she would look ahead at her dream for wanting to stop.

Within six weeks, Martha had quit smoking. She lost ten pounds. There was no room to eat on the kitchen table. And she divorced her husband. Said Martha, "I wanted to get rid of all the ashes in my life."

*

I was raised Catholic. One of the things I loved about it was Confession. You would tell the priest all of your sins and be forgiven. You got a fresh start.

We all need fresh starts. Lots of them. All the time. When you constantly look in your rearview mirror, you make it that much more difficult to create a new "you"—a you that wants to be ODD.

By the way, public-school kids never did understand Confession. One of them said, "You punch me in the head, you run off, and tell the priest your sins, now all's forgiven?"

I told him, "No, that's not the way it works at all. Punching a public-school kid in the head is not a sin."

An ODD View

BECOMING YOUR WIZARD OF ODD: Never make negative remarks especially to yourself about your past behavior. When you spend all your energy looking in your rearview mirror, you continually become who you have already been . . . again. Your ODD is "ahead" in your future, not in the "behind" of your rearview mirror.

BEING A WIZARD OF ODD TO OTHERS: Don't look at people in terms of who they have been but rather who they are, and, most important, who they want to become. Help them achieve their dreams.

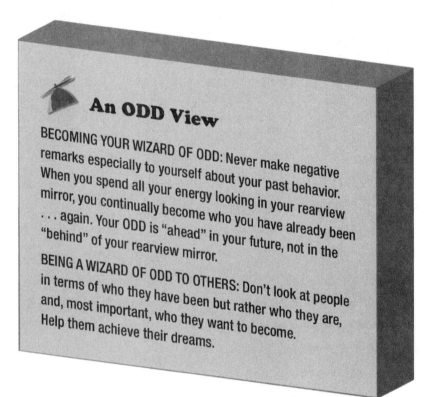

Becoming Your Own Coach

ODDS believe that if you *don't* talk to yourself, you're crazy.

They listen to the inner voice they have deliberately created—that inner voice, which stands outside of them and tells them they can do better, a lot better.

If you were fortunate, you had great parents, teachers and other adult influences in your young years who, rather than lock you into a straightjacket of expected behavior as defined by them, motivated you to find and live your ODD.

But as an adult, you don't have such people. Oh, you may have mentors who help you, but that is different from someone who takes a daily interest in guiding and enriching your life. You, and you alone, are now responsible for your inner guidance and strength that will lead you to your ODD.

You must develop that inner voice that stands outside of you and demands that you make that extra effort to push just a little harder, to exert yourself just a little longer, to become who you truly are. How do you do that? Where would that voice come from?

Think of the parent, teacher, coach, or boss who demanded that you give him or her nothing less than more of your very best. Now see that face and hear that voice again. When you are struggling to get to that next level, when life is pushing you down, when everyone tells you to give up, that you can't do it—that is when you listen to that voice from your past, which now lives in your heart.

An ODD View

BECOMING YOUR WIZARD OF ODD: Become your own coach by listening to the voices from your past that inspired and motivated you.

BEING A WIZARD OF ODD TO OTHERS: Are there people in your life you believe can do better? Talk to them. Ask them who has been the most motivating person in their life? What made that person so special? Why did they listen to that person? Ask them to listen to that person again.

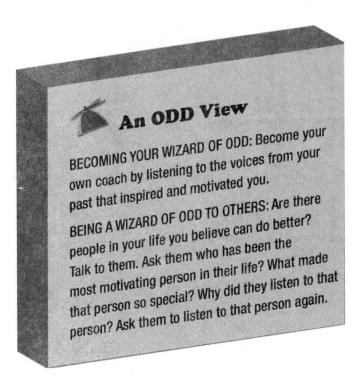

Pick Me Up, Carry Me

ODDS know that every age is about helping . . . and being helped.

When you raise a child, there are many versions before you get to the final edition. You begin with one so small you can hold it in your arms. The first few times I carried my daughter, it took her a while to realize I was not her mother. Nothing on me was edible.

But once I convinced my daughter that I was not part of her food chain, it was a good deal for both of us. She got to see the world from the same height as my eyes, and I got to see it with the same delight as hers. My daughter never did become a fan of the buggy. Who wants to look at life from the eye level of a collie?

She was an ideal companion. At weddings, we would dance together, cheek to cheek. I never once stepped on her feet.

Like all young creatures, she soon felt the urge to leave the nest. Every day, her feet would carry her to new adventures. But when the world became too sleepy . . . or too tough . . . tabletops that ran to the horizon, cups that took two hands to hold, voices yelling, "Don't do that!" she'd come running back to me holding her arms high. "Pick me up, pick me up, carry me."

My months were her millennia. I didn't hear her say, "Pick me up, carry me," very often anymore. But one night, when she was eleven and just too tired to walk, I carried her up two flights of stairs, which left me gasping for breath. She noticed.

"Not as strong as you used to be."

"Has it ever occurred to you that you're growing?"

Indeed, she was. Now when she said, "Pick me up," she meant, "Drive over here and pick me up."

I may live too long. It happens. Someday, she may look into my eyes and hear my silent prayer: "Pick me up. Carry me."

An ODD View

BECOMING YOUR WIZARD OF ODD: Being ODD is all about being strong. When you carry someone, you always get stronger.

BEING A WIZARD OF ODD TO OTHERS: Most of us are too proud to ask for help because we have been taught that it is a sign of weakness. We believe that it is ODD to ask for help. We are right. Be strong enough to be willing to lean on others.

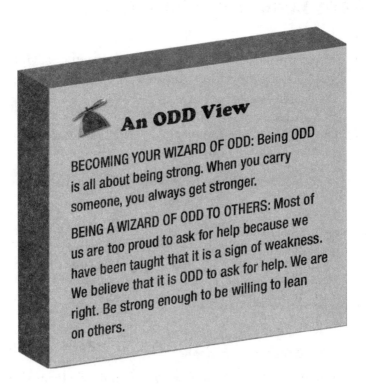

Friends

ODDS have great libraries. Living, breathing libraries.

David is a neighbor. Over the years, I've met quite a few of his friends. They are always fascinating people. I suggested to him that he have a party and invite all of them.

He said, "No, that wouldn't do at all. They'd probably kill each other."

"Why?"

"Because," said David, "the only thing they have in common is me. I learned from my mother how to choose friends. She believed that everyone is a book waiting to be read if only we'll take the time to read. A great library has all kinds of books. The same is true of a great library of friends.

"I have some friends who are extremely conservative while others are quite liberal. Some are funny. Some are not. I have rich friends and poor ones. Friends who rarely talk and others who never shut up. I have friends who can fix anything . . . and ones who can break anything.

"Among my friends are cynics and saints, athletes and couch potatoes, cops and crooks, fatties and skinnies, health nuts and just plain nuts.

"I have friends who have traveled all over the world and others who have never left their hometown. I have a friend who's a religious fanatic, another who's an atheist, and a third who's not quite sure. One friend has three Ph.D.s. Another never finished grammar school. But all of my friends are interesting."

David concluded, "Do I like everything about them? Of course not. But when you read a great book, do you rip out the pages you don't agree with?"

An ODD View

BECOMING YOUR WIZARD OF ODD: Every person is unique, ODD, and has lessons of life to share. Learn by reading them. In other words, listen.

BEING A WIZARD OF ODD TO OTHERS: Encourage them to build a great library.

Rain

An unseasonably hot, sweaty early June evening: A farmer sits on his tractor, watching his fields cough up dust. It hasn't rained in over two weeks, and he's worried. He's been walking a thin money line. A drought will force him into bankruptcy. His eyes don't spend more than a few moments on earth before they again begin scanning the sky for help. His lips constantly slip into silent prayers.

A few miles away, more prayers are being said. A boy stands on his back porch and looks up. The weather forecast on television is calling for rain, but the forecast has been wrong before. He has a baseball game tonight and it's the first one of the season that his father will be able to attend. The boy knows his father is going to be so proud when he hits that home run . . . he knows he'll hit one . . . if only it doesn't rain.

Teenage girls are praying, too. Prom night. "What if it rains? My hair! My dress!"

A small traveling circus, sponsored by the Chamber of

Commerce, has just finished setting up in the shopping mall's parking lot. The roadies don't even bother looking toward the sky as they string up the tents. Doesn't matter one way or the other to them.

There are parents doing some passionate praying. They're the ones who are foolish enough to tell their young children they are going to the circus tonight.

On the interstate, a truck driver is praying that the storm holds off for at least a little while. He's already way behind schedule. His foot squeezes down on the gas pedal.

The sky is speckled with puny puffs of white, but quickly moving in is a gang of deep-gray clouds with serious expressions on their faces. Within a few moments, they have crowded up the sky, pushing and shoving at one another. Angers of lightning flash among them.

In an instant, the day's breath has changed from musty to misty.

At the park district swimming pool, the four lifeguards on duty, in a move that seems almost choreographed, simultaneously stand up from their perched seats and start ordering the swimmers out of the water.

A newly married couple, who had just stepped out of their apartment building to take a walk, head back inside and go up the stairs to their apartment.

Streetlights are called to early duty as the deep metal gray of the sky closes over the earth.

The vanguard, a few fat drops, splatter their announcement. They barely beat the mob hurtling behind them.

The farmer stands just inside his barn door, smiling as the spray gently licks his face.

The young boy watches the storm from his kitchen window and listens to his father tell him that there will be other nights and other games.

Prom curls unravel. Some girls laugh. Some cry.

Some parents of young children are putting on their own circus in the basement. Others are sitting with their kids on their laps, looking out the living-room window, marveling at the storm. Then there are those who are yelling at their children that if they don't quit whining, they will never go to a circus.

On the interstate, the truck skids out of control and slams into an abutment. Being behind schedule will never again be a problem.

A young girl stands in the lobby of the park district building waiting for her mother to pick her up. She had prayed that the storm would not come. She loves swimming and wants to be an Olympic champion. She barely notices the small cramp in the back of her leg. She will never know that perhaps she was only a few moments away from drowning when the rains came.

The young couple isn't watching the rain at all. But the newest unborn member of the next generation will always love storms.

A little rain can change a lot of lives.

We share the same world, but we do not share the same lives.

Prayers are trying to push the clouds around.

An ODD View

BECOMING YOUR WIZARD OF ODD: Always celebrate the uniqueness of your life.

BEING A WIZARD TO OTHERS: See and share the world that Evens live in, too. But always keep your ODD point of view.

There Is No Such Thing as Equal Opportunity

ODDS know that. Everyone knows that. Such a silly term—"equal opportunity."

A friend of mine said, "If there was truly equal opportunity, then half this nation would be movie stars and the other half would be professional athletes."

ODDs thrive in an atmosphere of freedom. We Americans pride ourselves on living in a free society. But in a truly free society, you can never have "equal opportunity," because we're not equal. Some of us are smarter, more talented, harder working, or luckier.

Most parents spend most of their time trying to give their children an edge in life. That is the exact opposite of equal opportunity. What if a child does not have the good luck to have such parents? Unfortunate. Regardless, some of those children grow up, go out, and conquer the world anyway.

How do they do it? In this nation, for the most part, we do have equal rights, which is a very different thing from equal opportunity. Each of us has the right to pursue whatever we want as long as we don't encroach upon anyone else's right to do likewise.

The most common excuse for people who are not living their ODD is that "Life's not fair." Oh, really?

The passion to lose weight is given up because "I gain weight easier than other people. It's just not fair." The desire to earn a college degree is abandoned because "I have to spend more time studying than the other students. I'm not as smart as them. It's not fair." A career goal dies because "My boss doesn't like me. It's just not fair." Personal relationships unravel because "I'm too busy to spend more time with my friends and family. It's not fair."

Every one of these statements might be true. So what? All it means is that, if you're one of these people, you're going to have to diet longer, study harder, spend more time figuring out how to either get on the good side of your boss or getting a new one, and becoming more efficient with your use of time so that you can spend the proper amount of it with the people who are important to you.

No, life's not fair, and for a simple reason: none of us is exactly the same. We are all ODD.

In order for life to be fair, we'd all have to be born of the same parents at the same time; be the same height, weight, color, and sex; have the same intelligence and talents; and look exactly alike right down to the last dimple. That's just for starters.

Then we'd all have to live in the exact same house, go to the same school, sit in the same seat, get the same grades, go to the same places, and think and say the same things.

As we grew older, we'd have to have the same friends and lovers, parent the same children, like the same foods, play the same sports, and choose the same careers.

If one of us suffered an illness or accident, we'd all have to experience the same illness and accident in the exact same way.

If one of us won the lottery, we'd all win the lottery—same numbers, same amount of money, and on the same day.

We'd all die at the same moment in the very same way in the same exact bed.

If all of us were exactly alike, in every way, then life would be fair. It would also be boring and ridiculous. So is the idea of "equal opportunity."

"Equal" is an artificial sweetener.

An ODD View

BECOMING YOUR WIZARD OF ODD: Live a life that reflects the reality that there is no such thing as equal opportunity, only equal rights.

BEING A WIZARD OF ODD TO OTHERS: Encourage inequality based on merit.

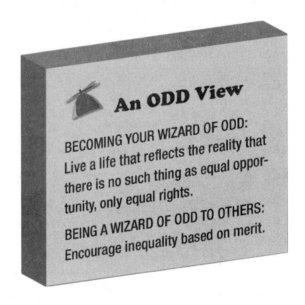

We Should Never Deny Ourselves the Agony of Defeat

Some people seem to think you shouldn't do anything unless you're really good at it. They don't understand that when you struggle to do something at which you clearly have no talent, you learn invaluable lessons. Humility for one. For another, it widens your horizons. If you stick to what you're good at and do only what you know, you'll never know anything else.

I'm lucky. I stink at a lot of things. I never did learn how to swim. A few years ago, on a family vacation, my daughter and I were taking scuba lessons at the hotel swimming pool. About twenty of us were lined up, in full equipment, getting ready to jump in. The instructor walked up to just me.

"Hey," he asked, "You do know how to swim?" When I said no, he said, "What are you? Nuts? You can't go scuba diving."

I asked, "Why not? I always end up at the bottom of the pool."

Learning is about doing new things, thinking new thoughts, going new places, and meeting new people. It's taking chances. That's risky. But remember, if you haven't lost, you haven't lived.

An ODD View

BECOMING YOUR WIZARD OF ODD: When you do something new, it's usually a struggle. But remember, each time you do it, it becomes a little less "new," and, therefore, easier to do.

BEING A WIZARD OF ODD TO OTHERS: Create an atmosphere where people are encouraged and praised for pushing the envelope rather than for sealing it.

Fun Is the Perfect Prayer

ODDs know that having fun is the perfect prayer. It's taking a bite out of life and saying, "Ah, just right."

ODDs realize that you don't have to go looking for sadness. It will find you. Illness, accidents, and other tragedies are just part of the price of being on the planet. It's the fun you have to create.

If you are ODD, you love who you are and you love what you do. Certain people are just not going to like you. It's called envy.

But some people enjoy being miserable. They think their misery, whining about it, and dwelling on it gets them attention. Maybe it does. Whatever. Remember, they have just as much right to misery as you have to happiness. If you can't convert them, desert them and move on.

An ODD View

BECOMING YOUR WIZARD OF ODD: Don't be surprised if some people find your happiness annoying. Don't let their annoyance distract from your ODD. Don't get Even.

BEING A WIZARD OF ODD TO OTHERS: If someone you know is unhappy, listen to them. Learn from them. Do what you can to make their lives more enjoyable. Help them discover the qualities that make them ODD.

School Is School, Life Is Life

College. Freshman year. English class. The professor walked in with our first homework assignments, which were the essays we had written for him. He announced to us, "There is a brilliant writer among you. I have taught college English for over thirty-five years. I know great writing when I read it."

Of course, each of the forty-two of us was sitting there thinking, *It's me, it's me, it's me.*

He began reading the essay. Neither I nor virtually anyone else in that class had any idea what he was saying.

The essay had been written by the young woman sitting next to me. I said to her, "You weren't born in this country, were you? I mean, English is your second language, isn't it?"

She was shocked. "How did you know? I don't have any accent at all."

"Because," I replied, "anyone who has grown up here has never heard of half of those words."

He was an college English professor. He loved big words. That young woman ended up working for a large manufacturing company in management. Besides myself, two other people in that class became professional writers. One of us got a B in the class. The other two got Cs.

As a professional writer, I have learned that the trick is to paint beautiful images, not with big words, but rather by creatively using simple ones.

An ODD View

BECOMING YOUR WIZARD OF ODD: Don't draw conclusions, lessons, or analogies from one world and apply them to another. Treat each one for what it is—a new opportunity to learn and grow.

BEING A WIZARD OF ODD TO OTHERS: Remind others to do likewise. Example: "This company is family." No, it's not. It may have a family-like atmosphere and all the employees may feel very emotionally close to one another, but it's still a company. Families do not have to show a profit, are not replaced by foreign competition, or get bought out by other families. To be ODD is to look at a situation for what it really is.

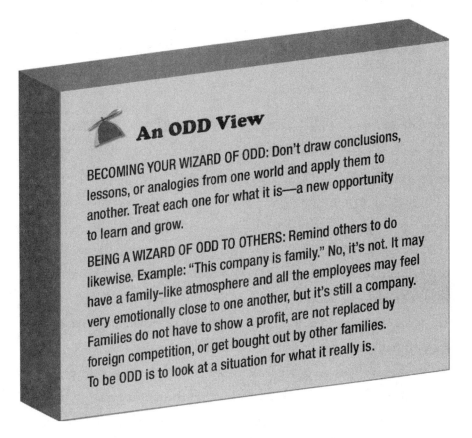

Who Are You Performing For?

Often, we do not live who we truly are because, unconsciously or otherwise, we are living lives designed to please other people. A simple way of finding out if this is true is to ask yourself a question you may have never asked before: "Who am I performing for?"

Shakespeare wrote, "All the world's a stage and all the men and women merely players." He is right, of course. The problem is, many times, we do not really think about who we are performing for, and how, by trying to please them, we are compromising our ODD.

Leo has made every choice in his life so that it would please his father. Leo chose his college, his career, and even the type of woman he married because he thought his father would approve. By the way, his father's been dead for twenty years.

Some of us are even performing for people we don't like. I know one fellow, for instance, whose wife divorced him when they were in their mid-twenties. These two people really did not like each other. Yet he spent the next thirty years living a life totally designed to impress her even though he never saw her again.

Alice was a sales rep who spent too much of her time "performing" for her support staff at the home office. She would devote inordinate amounts of energy making certain that she did not overburden or inconvenience any of them. In one sense, she was quite successful. Her support staff loved her. But her customers felt they were not getting enough attention and eventually left her, almost costing Alice her job.

When Alice looked out at the audience, who was she performing for? She should have seen her customers sitting in the first few rows. Her support staff should have been in the last few rows.

When you look past the stage lights, whose faces do you see? Is trying to please them encouraging you to pursue who you truly are and what you really want to do? If not, what can you do about it?

The higher you aim, the more often your audience, no matter who it is composed of, will tell you that you can't do it. In such matters, most people, most of the time, are wrong. It's "the majority rules," not "the majority's right." At one point, most people thought the world was flat. That didn't make it so.

As you live your daily life, when you look at your audience, shouldn't you see your family and your true friends? In the best seat in the house, shouldn't you see you?

An ODD View

BECOMING YOUR WIZARD OF ODD: Always be aware of who you are performing for.

BEING A WIZARD OF ODD TO OTHERS: If someone in your world seems confused, distracted, or depressed by their lives, ask him or her, "Who are you performing for?" That person may have never even thought about the question before.

The Journey Must Be as Exciting as the Destination

Some ways of life are so difficult to survive in that you only pursue them if you *need* to, not because you *want* to.

This is true of virtually all the professions in the entertainment industry. The girl who lives two doors down from me not only *wants* to be an actress, she *needs* to be an actress. She cannot imagine living her life any other way.

She has already begun paying the price for her dream. In the past year, she could not attend her prom because she had a small role in a community theater production. She had to skip a trip with her friends because she was taking acting lessons. Her mother, not her, told me about both incidents. In the girl's mind, she wasn't paying any price at all. When I asked her if missing such activities bothered her, she replied, "You know, I didn't really think about it. There was never any doubt in my mind as to what I wanted to do."

When I was a kid, my dream was to be a major league baseball player. As I've already mentioned, I had no talent. I spent years playing baseball and got nowhere. I played second string on my Little League team and couldn't even make my high school team.

Didn't matter. Every time I ran out onto the field, swung a bat, ran to a base, or caught a ball, it was its own reward. That's the way it is when you pursue your ODD dream. The journey is just as exciting as the destination.

A few years ago, a young man, who was familiar with my work as a novelist, asked me, "Do you think I should be a writer?"

"No."

He was both shocked and angered. "You've never even read anything I've written. Why would you say that?"

"Because you had to ask."

An ODD View

BECOMING YOUR WIZARD OF ODD: If it's truly your dream, the price you're paying never even enters your mind. Being ODD is its own reward.

BEING A WIZARD OF ODD TO OTHERS: ODD is a fire that yearns to spread. Just by being around someone like you, others will pursue their own dreams that much more intensely.

Killer Bones or Marvin

Cindy was telling me about her experience on jury duty. She said, "He was charged with armed robbery. The defendant's name was Killer Bones. We found him guilty."

I asked her, "The guy's name was actually Killer Bones?"

She said, "That's right. He had his name legally changed from Marvin to Killer Bones. To be honest, the evidence wasn't all that strong. Marvin probably would have beaten it. But Killer Bones?"

Marvin saw himself as a criminal and wanted other people to see him that way, too. So they did.

How do you see "you"?

Do you see yourself as a success or as a failure?

When you pursue your ODD, no matter how feeble the results, you should always focus on what you have accomplished rather than on what you have not. As long as you are pursuing who you are and what you want to do, you *are* a success.

Defining yourself as a failure will hurt you. "Failure" makes you feel bad about yourself and eats away at your self-confidence, which often causes depression. That, in turn, usually leads to inaction.

Only when you do nothing, when you are not even trying to pursue your ODD, are you truly a failure.

That feeling of success gets you thinking good thoughts about yourself. You experience a sense of joy, enthusiasm, and energy. You become passionate about who you are and what you do.

An ODD View

BECOMING YOUR WIZARD OF ODD: Do you see yourself as Marvin or Killer Bones? Earlier I said to listen to everyone's opinion but take no one's advice. That, however, does not excuse you from being ignorant of the signals you send out to other people indicating how you want to be perceived. If the vast majority of people you know see you as a duck, you should ask yourself why. Indeed, they may be wrong. But you should know the reason they are all making the same mistake.

BEING A WIZARD TO OTHERS: Encourage people to think about themselves in positive terms and to focus on what they accomplish rather than on what they do not accomplish. Do not tolerate negative remarks. They are the germs that can cause the death of any group or organization.

Count Your Blessings

Being a Wizard of ODD is not based on what you have, but on what you appreciate having. Here's an old proverb that is so true: "The richest person is not who has the most but who needs the least."

When you savor the ordinary things in life—a cup of coffee in the morning, a conversation with a friend, embracing a summer's heat or a winter's cold, driving down the street just watching the world go by, holding a child's hand or a lover's gaze—you can't help but love who you are and what you do.

Some of the happiest people I know are those with the least. They have lost so much, or they never had it to begin with, that they relish what they do have even more.

Most of us take the small miracles for granted, truly appreciating them only after they have left our lives. Most of us—not all of us. There are a few rare ones, like Carl, who always understood how truly blessed he was.

Years ago, Carl lived a few doors down from me. He worked

in the vegetable market, so he would be home every day in the early afternoon. Carl would then take a long walk around the neighborhood, often not returning until suppertime.

During that walk, he'd first visit the neighborhood shut-ins. He'd laugh with them, do their laundry, walk their dogs, cut their lawns, or cut their meat. Whatever.

He wouldn't laugh when he visited Mrs. Kaline. Carl and Mrs. Kaline both loved soap operas. She would videotape them in the morning so that she and Carl could cry together when he came over in the afternoon.

When school got out, Carl would be there to walk home with the children who lived near him. You would think that some kids would find an old man's company boring. But in Carl's case, you would be wrong. Carl was the only grown man I've ever known who truly found knock-knock jokes funny.

What really bothered me about Carl was that he was having so much fun. I didn't know anybody who was getting as much mileage out of life as Carl. So you see what I mean. The guy could really get on your nerves.

His favorite expression was "I have been truly blessed," which was somewhat different from mine at the time, "I have been truly cursed."

When he lost his job at the vegetable market, Carl said he was getting tired of the long bus ride anyway but just didn't have the courage to quit. "I'm glad it worked out this way," he said. "I have been truly blessed."

When Carl's only child, Bob, died instantly in a car crash at the age of thirty, Carl told me that he was so fortunate to have had his son for all those years. "Besides," said Carl, "he didn't have to suffer. I have been truly blessed."

Carl's wife had cancer for nearly four years before she passed away. In Carl's eyes, as usual, he was truly blessed. "We had time to say good-bye."

Carl lived into his early nineties and, eventually, became a shut-in himself. All his neighbors and his friends, including the ones who, as children, had walked home with him from school, came to visit. Carl would smile and laugh and listen as someone who is truly blessed would do.

The last time I saw Carl was in a nursing home. At ninety-three, his life was now within days of ending. An ice storm had knocked out the building's electricity. I could hear the emergency generators humming as they energized the nursing home's life-support systems. Unfortunately, for Carl, his television was not considered one of them.

When I walked into his darkened room, I hardly recognized the man. For the first time, I saw what he looked like when he wasn't smiling. Know anyone who always wears glasses? If you ever do see that person without those glasses, they actually look like someone else. Same thing.

Carl was staring at the blank television screen. I sat down next to his bed. I spoke lightheartedly so that Carl would know I was kidding, which, for the most part, I was.

"Carl, is it possible that you are finally having a lousy day?"

Carl turned slowly and stared at me, still unsmiling. "Yes, this is a lousy day." He looked out his window. The ice-covered branches seemed to be made of glass.

He repeated his words. "This is a lousy day. . . . But, you know, in ninety-three years, to have just one lousy day . . ." He was still staring out the window, but I could see the edges of a smile beginning to grow on his face. "Just one lousy day in all these years . . . I have been truly blessed."

I had to smile, too. "Carl, I give up."

Something Carl never did.

An ODD View

BECOMING YOUR WIZARD OF ODD: Feed your Wizard of ODD. Place a gift box, with an easily removable top, on the dresser in your bedroom. Put a stack of index cards next to it. On the days you're feeling good, write down on a card one of the gifts that life is giving you and toss it into the box. On the days you are feeling crummy, take a card out of the box and relish that gift.

BECOMING A WIZARD OF ODD TO OTHERS: Encourage them to be like Carl.

What Is Your View from the Mountain?

ODDS know that the only things in life that are black and white are the colors black and white.

I was driving with Donna to a meeting with a major corporation in downtown Chicago. She worked as a clerical assistant in one of their branch offices. Since I was going by her office, I offered to give her a ride, which she gladly accepted.

She said to me, "I hate it when they hold these meetings downtown."

"Why?"

"Because," she replied, "normally, I have to drive my own car, and the parking is very expensive, about twenty dollars."

"Don't they reimburse you?"

"Oh, yes, they give me a check at the end of the month. But I need the twenty dollars now."

The president of that company is a friend of mine. I told him this story. He was shocked. He had always prided himself on running an employee-friendly company. The problem was that he is a wealthy man. Twenty dollars means nothing to him. He didn't realize that it could mean so much to someone else.

The next time a meeting was held downtown, he stood at the door with twenty-dollar bills and handed them to anyone who had paid for their own parking.

An ODD View

BECOMING YOUR WIZARD OF ODD: If you're living on top of the mountain, make it a habit to travel down to the bottom so that you can look up and get a clear view of you.

BEING A WIZARD OF ODD TO OTHERS: When you're down from the mountain's peak, teach anyone who wants to learn how to climb.

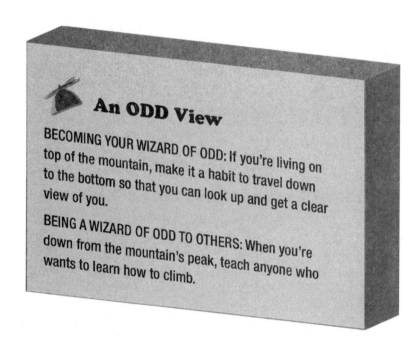

Talk to Strangers

ODDS believe the world is a sea of chaos, each day bringing a new wave of opportunities.

Your ODD grows hotter from new ideas. New ideas come from new people. Despite what your parents told you, talk to strangers.

As a professional speaker, I spend a lot of time traveling alone. If I didn't talk to strangers, most of the time I wouldn't talk to anyone at all.

I've had wonderful conversations with people I've never spoken to before or since. Usually, I'm standing in line. I get bored so I talk to somebody. I don't care about their age, sex, color, where they're from, or what they've done. If they're standing next to me, I talk.

Strangers, unlike people who deal with each other all the time, can often discuss delicate topics mainly because they don't know each other. Nothing's at stake.

Talking to strangers is always an exercise in discipline for me. I love to talk . . . I am a professional speaker. But with strangers, once I get the conversation rolling, I try to keep my mouth shut. After all, I've already heard everything I have to say.

Late one night, I flew into Atlantic City to do a presentation the following morning.

I didn't get to the hotel until nearly midnight. But because the hotel had casinos, the restaurants were still open. Standing in line waiting to be seated, I got into a conversation with an older woman who was standing behind me. I can't remember how the conversation began, but I know I started it. At some point, she asked, "Are you having dinner alone?" I told her that I was. She said, "I'm a high-roller. The casino is always giving me comps. I have two tickets for dinner tonight. Why don't you join me?" So I did.

It turned out that this lady spent over twenty years working in various countries throughout the Middle East. She gave me a history and a political analysis of that area of the world, which was fascinating. But I would have missed it all if I hadn't talked to a stranger.

Because I travel so much, many of the strangers I talk to are cab drivers. A few years ago, I commented to one, "There seem to be a lot of banks around here."

"Oh, yeah," he agreed, "this town is mostly banks and churches. The big shots spend all week stealing and then go to church on Sunday and pray for forgiveness."

Another time, I was sitting in the airport. The flight was delayed. I was going nuts. I had to be in Boston within the next few hours, but it didn't look like it was going to happen.

I got into a conversation with the fellow next to me. At some point he said, "I used to be like you."

"What do you mean?"

"Getting really upset over something that I had no control over anyway. I was working eighteen-hour days, running five different companies. Making a lot of money and spending all of it. One day, I'm having lunch with my business partner. He stopped talking and stared at me. It took me a few seconds to realize he was dead. Massive heart attack.

"That moment ended his life and changed mine. I got rid of four of the companies and now, every morning when I get up, I tell myself—'Today is going to be fun'—and I make sure it is."

I said, "You don't understand. I have a presentation to do in Boston tomorrow morning."

He replied, "Don't kid yourself. If you don't get there, they'll survive."

"Yeah, but I'll lose money. . . ."

"You know," he replied, "my mother always said that if money can solve it, then it's not a real problem. A year from today, will any of this make a difference in your life?"

"Ah . . . I guess not."

He got up. "I'm going to get some ice cream. Want some?"

"Absolutely."

Strangers are a vast and usually ignored source of information, laughs, insight, and experiences. After all, think about all the friends you have. The first time you talked to them, weren't they strangers?

An ODD View

BECOMING YOUR WIZARD OF ODD: Talk to strangers . . . then listen to them.

BEING A WIZARD OF ODD TO OTHERS: How well do you know the people you deal with every day? Encourage them to talk about themselves. Ask yourself, "Are most of the people I 'know' actually strangers?"

Wishing Is for Wimps

Some people are fond of saying, "I wish . . ." "I wish I had a different job." "I wish I lived somewhere else." "I wish I had a better marriage . . ."

Wishing is for young children standing by a fountain with a few cents in their hands and adults who don't even have that much in their heads. When you use the word "wish," you are telling yourself that you have no control over the situation, and that is never true.

About a year ago, Thomas, a truly ODD guy, discovered that he had a life-threatening illness. He told me, "My first responses were, like most people I suppose, panic, depression, and asking, 'Why me?' Then I asked, 'Why not me?' So I sat down and created a game plan to deal with the situation.

"The moment I began doing that I felt control over my life flowing back to me. I know that I am in for, literally, the fight of my life. I can only do my best. I cannot control the world." Thomas pointed to his head. "But I can control my world."

An ODD View

BECOMING YOUR WIZARD OF ODD: "When you wish upon a star . . ." Well, that's a nice way to spend a moment but hardly the basis for putting ODD in your life. ODD is action.

BEING A WIZARD OF ODD TO OTHERS: When someone makes a wish, ask them what specific steps they can take that will increase the probability their wish will come true. Suggest they write down those steps. You have now helped that person create a goal that can be pursued and achieved by living a life that is uniquely theirs.

When You Love Your Neighbor, You Love Yourself

We are 99 percent alike. We all want basically the same things: happiness, good health, a safe and loving world for our children to grow up in, and the freedom to live our lives the way we choose.

Ah, but that 1 percent difference is what makes each of us special. Our ODD lives in that 1 percent.

You can know someone their entire life and they'll still surprise you. In fact, if you take yourself beyond your own 99 percent—meet new people, do new things, go new places, and explore your own unique 1 percent—you'll even begin surprising yourself.

The 1 percent difference—that's where all the learning and fun occurs. That's where we learn from one another. That's where our ODD thrives. How dull life would be if we were all alike.

The great sadness is that some of us, instead of enjoying our differences, use them as reasons for discrimination, outright hatred, and even violence.

I have met a number of supremacists—racial, religious, and even sexual. They all have two things in common. First, they are always members of the group that's supposedly "supreme." Second, they are never good examples of their own theory.

Sometimes, there is simply too much antagonism in people's hearts to allow them to love their neighbors. Fine. Then tolerate them. You don't have to love or even like someone to live in harmony with them. But you do have to remind yourself that they have just as much right to their views as you do to yours. Agree to disagree.

An ODD View

BECOMING YOUR WIZARD OF ODD: Love your neighbor. There is something very wrong with you if you don't like 99 percent of yourself.

BEING A WIZARD OF ODD TO OTHERS: Be totally intolerant of intolerance among your group. You cannot control how people think or feel, but you can control how they act. If someone in your group harbors hatred in their heart, make it clear they have a choice: fake it or get out.

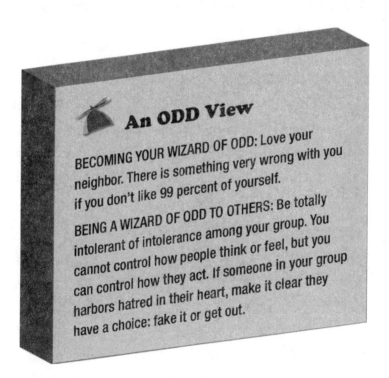

Watch What Your Mind Eats

Maybe it's because it's more obvious to us when our bodies get out of shape than when our minds do, but we seem to give a lot more attention to what we eat rather than to what we think.

Spiritually, we survive on a diet of junk-food words: negative, nasty, and bad news. If the media isn't telling us about crime, crookedness, international havoc, or the meaningless drivel about famous people, its commercials are harping at us for being too fat, too poor, too ugly, or too sober.

The media's even gotten into the habit of reporting "big stories" that aren't big at all. How many storm warnings have ended up drizzles?

Then there are people in our everyday lives who, all too frequently, make disparaging remarks.

Worst of all, our own voices and minds are often whining about the weather, what we don't have, what we should have, what we do have, and what we don't want.

The ODDs I have met seem to fall into one of three categories.

First of all, there are those, like Carl, who just seem to be born happy. Maybe it's a yet-to-be-discovered gene buried deep within their DNA, which tells them that they are special and life is grand. That's how they see it. That's how they live it.

Then there are those of whom misfortune has landed a solid punch to their spirits—losing a job, a life-threatening disease, the death of a loved one. The tragedy causes them to look at life in a new way—where every moment is a kaleidoscope of laughter and love.

Then there are people like me. I'm the most cynical, whining, negative person you'd ever want to meet . . . or not meet. I have to work at improving my mental attitude every day. Some days, I win. Some days, I lose.

In many ways, I'm like a recovering alcoholic. When an alcoholic stops drinking, he's still an alcoholic. He's just one who's no longer drinking. When I'm a positive, upbeat, love-the-world guy, I'm still a whiner. I'm just a whiner who's choosing to be ODD.

Some people would call that being a phony. Better to be a phony than an annoyance. A friend of mine, Carol Kleiman, like most of us, has her good days and her bad. But whenever you ask her how she's doing, she always replies, "I'm perfect and getting better."

If we want to be ODD, we must make a conscious effort to feed our minds healthy foods—read motivational books, think positive thoughts, and hang around with ODD people while avoiding the verbal garbage that is constantly being thrown at us.

If you're like me, there's a great book you should read, *How to Stop Worrying and Start Living,* by Dale Carnegie. It's an old book so the examples are dated. Doesn't matter. It's wonderful. Since it's an old book, it might be hard to find. It's worth the effort—a gourmet meal for the mind.

An ODD View

BECOMING YOUR WIZARD OF ODD: Someone much wiser than I said, "You are what you think all day long. How could it be otherwise?" For just one day, count both the negative and the positive remarks you make. The next day, make your mind eat a healthy diet.

BEING A WIZARD OF ODD TO OTHERS: Don't tolerate negative comments from people around you. Even criticism can be expressed in positive, constructive ways. Give positive energy to those around you. Demand it from them.

Live a Rainbow Life

Some of us don't live ODD lives, because we do a lousy job of finding out what will truly make us happy.

Sometimes, what you love finds you. Timothy, who is a neighbor of mine, is a brilliant carpenter. He knew he would be a carpenter when he was five years old and had picked up his first piece of wood. He was accepted to medical school but turned it down to live his passion. Timothy talks about wood the way many men talk about women—the beauty, the sleek lines, the personality . . .

But, more often than not, you have to find the passion that makes you ODD.

We live in a rainbow world, but, day after day, we choose gray. Every morning, we get up and wear the same kind of clothes, eat the same kinds of foods, go to the same places, talk to the same people, and say the same things.

Why? Because we choose to live a predictable life rather than an ODD one. It's safer. But isn't it better to be excited than complacent? Isn't it better to be challenged than resigned? Isn't it better to be scared than bored?

Many people are so afraid of feeling excited or happy or sad or anything at all that they live the same day over and over again until the numbness that engulfs them becomes an acceptable substitute for life.

The irony is that this "security" they seek is pure illusion, especially in today's fast-changing world. Such people believe they have jobs that will last forever . . . until the day their job no longer exists. They believe their marriage will last forever, but it doesn't. They believe they'll live forever, but they don't.

If you want to see people who truly have security, go to the cemetery. There are rows and rows of them.

You will hear a child say, "I hate spinach."

"Ever taste it?"

"No."

"Then how do you know you hate it?"

"I just know."

Some of us never grow up. We avoid most of life's adventures because of "I just know."

Studies have shown that most people read, not to discover new ideas, but rather to confirm the ones they already have.

When I was a freshman in college, I had to take one of three courses—math, science, or anthropology. I knew what the first two were. I had done miserably in both of them in high school. So I took the devil I didn't know, anthropology. I loved it. But I would have never discovered that if I had not, in a way, been forced to take it.

Sometimes, we should do something simply because we have not done it before. If you're the kind of person who every week reads *Time Magazine,* this week read the *National Enquirer*. If nothing else, you'll get the news three weeks early.

An ODD View

BECOMING YOUR WIZARD OF ODD: Life is learning and learning is life. Always be getting better at something. Live all the colors of your rainbow.

BEING A WIZARD OF ODD TO OTHERS: Tell them, "Find friends who are not mirrors of you. If you're young, find some friends who are old. If you're conservative, find liberal ones. If you read a book with a point of view, make sure it's one with which you disagree. Every day, do something new even if it's as simple as talking to a neighbor you've never spoken to before. Life offers a large menu. Try new entrées. Stop ordering the same thing."

Gatekeepers

If you're ODD, you are going to encounter lots of gatekeepers. They are the ones you have to get past to reach the next level. One way or another, perhaps just for a moment, they are your bosses and they pass judgment on you.

The problem is that your true audience is the one that's on the other side of the gatekeepers. Their tastes may be very different from the gatekeeper's. Your audience may love what you are doing. But they, and you, will never know if you do not get past the gatekeepers.

Gatekeepers can be so strong they create their own reality. At a college lecture for journalism students, an editor of a major newspaper was asked to define news. He replied, "If I choose to print it, then it is news. If I don't, then it's not."

But, quite often, gatekeepers are wrong. Read about successful people. The vast majority of them were repeatedly stopped by gatekeepers until they managed to get past them and reach their goal. For instance, the book series, Chicken Soup for the Soul, the publishing phenomenon of the twentieth century, was turned down by at least thirty-five different editors. Thirty-five different people who were paid to recognize books that the public would want to buy said, "No."

An ODD View

BECOMING YOUR WIZARD OF ODD: Try to please the gatekeepers in your life because it is easier that way, but don't do it at the expense of not giving your audience what you truly believe it wants. If you cannot get past the gatekeepers, then just jump over the fence.

BEING A WIZARD OF ODD TO OTHERS: Support those you believe in who are trying to get past the gatekeepers.

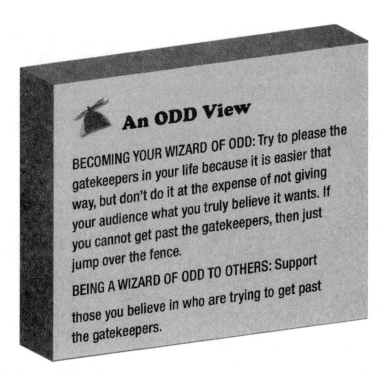

Who's Responsible? Who Cares?

Ernie is not a very happy fellow. He spends a lot of his energy dwelling on all the people "responsible" for making his life so crummy.

Indeed, Ernie has had his share of rotten influences. Ernie's father deserted the family when Ernie was barely two. His mother was an alcoholic who loved her drinking more than her children. Ernie had numerous teachers stereotype him as a troublemaker, so he became one.

What Ernie does not seem to understand is that although these various individuals may be responsible for his sorry state, they are not paying the price for it. Ernie is. It is Ernie who has low self-esteem. It is Ernie who is wasting so much of his time looking back at who is "responsible" rather than accepting the truth that he, not they, is daily paying the price and that the only way he is going to stop is to let go of his past and focus on his future—to find the ODD in his life.

An ODD View

BECOMING YOUR WIZARD OF ODD: Who's responsible? Who cares? Enjoy your suffering for a moment and then move on. Why constantly relive it? Learn from the past. Don't tie up your hands for the future by holding grudges.

BEING A WIZARD OF ODD TO OTHERS: Do you know people who are using injustices from their past as crutches for their present? People who are allowing the past to drain the energy from their lives? Encourage them to focus on what can be, not what has been. Point out to them who is really paying the price. Help them to live their ODD now.

How Many Feet Do You Need?

For many of us, two feet are not enough to stand on. We need everyone else's feet too.

A friend of mine owns a farm. One day, I was visiting him. He opened a gate to let about forty sheep into the field. Before he let them through, he stuck a stick between the two posts of the gate, eighteen inches off the ground. The first few sheep jumped over it. Then he took the stick away. The sheep that followed kept jumping over the stick that wasn't there.

Do you leap over sticks that are not there just so you can be one of the crowd?

Pursuing your ODD is supposed to make you happy. If it makes others happy too, that's nice. Nice, but not necessary.

You cannot completely be who you are and what you are if you do not unconditionally love yourself. The alternative is handing control of your life over to the conditional love of others. That is, you allow your actions to be dictated by emotional threats, virtually always unspoken, from those around you. "I'll love you if you behave the way I think you should."

Do you want people in your life who are there only because you're living according to their dictates?

Others will either respect you or reject you for being your own person. That's their choice.

Take the time to get to know yourself. You'll like you, and you'll decide that you deserve a life of ODD. And nothing less.

An ODD View

BECOMING YOUR WIZARD OF ODD: The essence of ODD is living your life the way you choose, standing on your own two feet.

BEING A WIZARD OF ODD TO OTHERS: Give others the same freedom you desire. Help them find their ODD, not deny it.

ODDs Are Grateful

Want to stand out from the crowd? Be different? Remembered? Known as an outstanding employer, sensational employee, terrific customer, great parent, wonderful student, super human being? ODD? Show gratitude.

A story from an ODD fellow: Last week, my boss and I went out to dinner. We've done that a few dozen times during the past years. But this time, when the check came, I told him I would pay for it. He reacted the way I thought he would.

"Oh, no, that's not necessary. I'll put it on the expense account."

But I insisted. "You always take care of dinner, and this is my small way of thanking you."

I didn't pay for dinner to "get ahead." I already am ahead. I did it because it made me feel good.

The next day, I found out that it also made my boss feel good.

He came into my office and said to me, "Thanks. You know, when you're the person in charge, people forget that, just like everybody else, you like to be appreciated. Bosses are human beings, too."

An ODD View

BECOMING YOUR WIZARD OF ODD: Show gratitude. My dad often said to me, "You can never say, 'Thank you,' too often."

BEING A WIZARD OF ODD TO OTHERS: Tell them what my mother told me: Every month, write a letter to someone who matters and tell them why. Not a phone call. Not an e-mail. A letter. Be grateful.

Sacred Time

It takes focus to find and live your ODD.

Today, we all have a "remote control" mentality. In this modern, fast-paced world, most of us have lost the ability to concentrate, to focus for any length of time on any one thing including our ODD.

For instance, the average person receives over 3,500 messages a day. There are so many demands for our attention that it tends to skip from one stimulus to the next.

We cannot get our minds to sit still long enough so that we can organize our thoughts to get where we want to go.

The typical television viewer now has an attention span of about three seconds. People who create TV programming know this. That's why so many shows today begin with the actual program rather than the theme song and credits. Television producers realize that if they don't grab your attention within the first three seconds, you'll click to another channel.

In fact, how many times have you been in a conversation with someone and wished you had a remote control so you could switch to somebody more interesting?

Many people have come to do with their lives what they do with their television's remote control: they skip from one moment to the next. They have no patience with their jobs, their business associates, friends, their mates, or creating a game plan that will help them live their ODD.

The solution: Create a moment in your day called Sacred Time during which you focus on what you believe is important. It may only be a few minutes. But block out everything else. No phone calls, no conversations, no music blaring.

You might choose to use this Sacred Time to reevaluate the direction your life is taking. You may ask yourself, "What are the truly important goals in my life? What am I doing to achieve them?" Write down your conclusions even if it's just a few words. Do it every day. You'll be amazed at your progress.

Alice, a single mother, has designated 6:30 to 7:30 every evening as the Sacred Time she shares solely with her child. She told me, "I can't do it every night. Sometimes, something comes up that I have to take care of. But since I've created Sacred Time, I'm spending far more quality time with my child than I ever have before."

Tom runs a multimillion dollar corporation. His Sacred Time is 7:00 to 7:45 every morning at his desk before anyone else arrives at work. He first analyzes his previous day's activities. Then Tom plans his upcoming day and reviews his long-term goals. Tom said, "I often get more accomplished in that forty-five minutes than I do in a day full of meetings."

An ODD View

BECOMING YOUR WIZARD OF ODD: Creating Sacred Time gives you the ability to focus on both living and achieving what makes you ODD.

BEING A WIZARD OF ODD TO OTHERS: If you are in a position to influence others, Sacred Time can change you from someone who is constantly "putting out fires," to a leader who instills in his or her colleagues that desire to achieve their ODD.

But I H-A-T-E What I'm Doing

Even if you believe that, at least for the moment, you have to do something you hate, discovering the ODD in it or your ODD in it will help make whatever it is more rewarding. How to find your ODD in it?

- ➡ Remind yourself that you *do not* have to do this. You always have a choice to do something else. Why did you make this one? In all probability, it was to get to a better place in your life.
- ➡ Think about where you are going and not about where you are.
- ➡ Make it a game. This may take some creative thinking on your part, but it will be worth it. For instance, if there is a particular activity you despise, how fast can you get it done? Time yourself. Always be striving to set a new world's record. Or is there simply a more interesting way to do it?
- ➡ No matter what you are doing, in some ways, somehow, it is

enriching other people's lives. Focus on how you are making it a better world for all of us.

- ➡ If you are making money by doing this activity, focus on how that money is going to make your life and perhaps the lives of those around you better.
- ➡ Savor all the little miracles that are blessing your day. Christopher Reeve, who became a quadriplegic because of a horse-riding accident, once said, "What I'd give to walk into a kitchen one morning and pour cereal into a bowl."
- ➡ Think of the activity you like most about your job and then realize how all the other things you do feed into it.
- ➡ If you are working as part of a team, try to be the strongest member of that team. How can you help the other members?
- ➡ Don't do things that enhance your misery such as watching the clock or constantly complaining or dogging it.

An ODD View

BECOMING YOUR WIZARD OF ODD: Remind yourself that, sometimes, to get where you want to go, you have to begin where you don't want to be.

BEING A WIZARD OF ODD TO OTHERS: If someone around you is unhappy doing what he or she is doing, try to make that person feel better. One way may be sharing some of the ideas you have just read here.

Mentors

ODDS know that life is a continuum of learning and teaching. Find mentors. Be a mentor.

Wherever you want to be, someone is already there. Talk to them. Listen to them. Learn from them. They will be flattered that you asked their advice and will be more than willing to teach you.

Wherever you are, someone wants to be there. Teach them. Help them. When you share your knowledge, your experiences, and your feelings, your spirit will grow. It is a law of nature.

I never truly realized how important mentoring was until my daughter was born. Within seconds of her birth, I held her in my arms. At that moment, for the first time, I thought about all the gifts that I had received from those who had shared their lives with me. A few hours after her birth, I wrote my daughter a letter.

Dear Child of Mine,

As I look into your eyes for the very first time, I cannot begin to understand the emotions that are gushing within my soul. I don't know you at all. How could

I? You are only twenty minutes old. In an hour, you will live another three lifetimes. Yet, already, I love you differently and more deeply than anyone I've ever loved before. I would die for you.

Birthdays are about presents so, on this very first birthday, let me give you gifts that will last as long as I live.

I give you the gift of freedom. Every moment of your infancy, every moment of your childhood, and, certainly, every moment of your teenage years, you will be moving away from me. That's the way it should be. At first, the movements will be so small I won't even notice them. But, one day, I'll look up, see the distance between us, and wonder why I never saw it before. And it will only continue to grow until that day arrives when, for the first time, you truly walk out of my sight. Come back because you want to, not because you have to.

I give you the gift of rejoicing in who you are and not who I want you to be. I will remind myself that I'm not raising a mirror. You are not here to grasp what was beyond my reach. You are not here to complete my unfulfilled dreams. You are not here to live my life again. You are here to celebrate your existence in the way you choose.

I give you the gift of me. All of me. In my mind, you'll never be more than a thought away. My ears will hear your whispers, your sighs, your laughter, your cries, your triumphs, and your tragedies.

My eyes will try to see the world as you see it: young, exciting, loving.

You'll hear my voice even if I cannot speak—teaching you, encouraging you, guiding you, correcting you, and reminding you how special you are.

My shoulder is there for you to lean on.

My arms will always long to hug you, to carry you where you want to go, to hold you back when I know I must, to let you go when I know I should.

My hands will pat you on the back, applaud your efforts, and nudge you in the direction we both believe is true.

Hopefully, my feet will leave footprints that you will want to follow, but won't run after you when you want to leave.

And every day, you'll give me the gifts of being who you are, doing what you do, living your life the way you choose.

Like all gifts, mine are free. You don't owe me anything. But perhaps, one day, years from now, you'll take these gifts, rewrap them in your own special way, and give them to the new life you will hold in your arms.

Dear Child of Mine, Happy Birth Day.

An ODD View

BECOMING YOUR WIZARD OF ODD:
Love yourself.

BEING A WIZARD OF ODD TO OTHERS.
Remember, you are never truly an adult until you consider all the children of the world yours.

Each of us
is a rock that sends ripples
through generations.

For Further Information

For further information on John R. Powers, Ph.D., his keynote addresses, seminars, and workshops, please visit his website at www.johnpowerspmi.com, contact him at johnpowerspmi@aol.com, or call his office at (262) 249-8622.

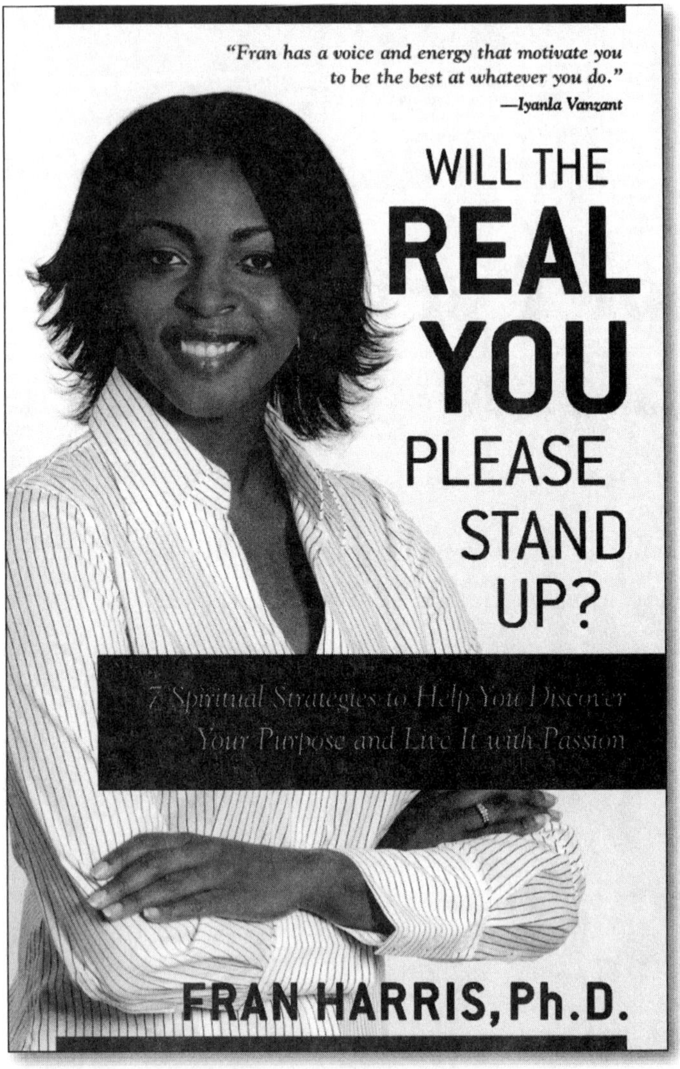
"Fran has a voice and energy that motivate you to be the best at whatever you do."
—Iyanla Vanzant
WILL THE
REAL
YOU
PLEASE
STAND
UP?
7 Spiritual Strategies to Help You Discover Your Purpose and Live It with Passion
FRAN HARRIS, Ph.D.

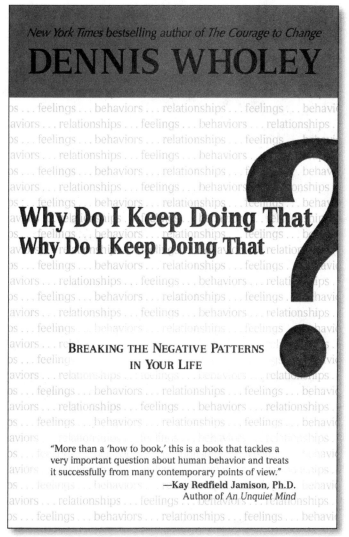

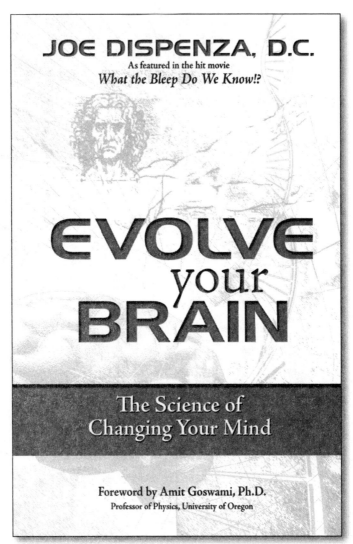

Those who thirst for
recognition from others
don't recognize
much in themselves.

I am like a
California redwood.
I gather strength
from those around me.

Life is a gift;
this is supposed
to be fun.

I am odd.
I love who I am.
I love what I do
or I will do
something else.

Odd is the
starting point.
Journey is the
destination.

Every moment
on this planet
is a privilege.

Today is a
once-in-a-lifetime
opportunity.

Never walk a road
that doesn't lead
to your heart.

Evens go with the flow.
Odds have the courage
to ride the waves.

Losing and learning
to go on and live again
is the only kind of
winning that truly matters.

The trouble with
going nowhere
is that it takes forever
to get there.

When I don't know
what I want to do
I begin with knowing
what I *don't* want to do.

If I'm odd does that
make us even?
–yes–

I can either learn
from someone or judge them,
but I can't do both.
One eliminates the possibility
of the other.

No one has
power over me
unless I choose
to give it to them.

I never confuse
succeeding and failing
with winning and losing.

While nothing is wrong
with having to start over,
There is everything wrong
with not starting at all.

Hope is the joy
of planning for,
but not knowing,
the future.

I am a love-a-holic,
not a work-a-holic.

I see the person
and not the sliver.

I am a wizard;
I give people faith
in themselves.

I'm wiser today
than I was yesterday;
I will be wiser tomorrow.

Evens
get ready . . .
get set . . .
Odds go.

Rules are the answers to
yesterday's questions.
We need guidelines.

An odd's heartbeat
is passion.

Rewarding mediocrity
gets more of it.

Help those who need it;
reward those who deserve it.

Odds lead with
their strengths
and work on
their weaknesses.

I am strong enough
to lean on others.

A bonfire is
lighter than a candle;
hang around with other odds.

Odds know
the difference between
"explanations" that seek
solutions and "excuses"
that pass the blame.

If I haven't lost,
I haven't lived.

Wishing is
for wimps.

An odd's definition of
self-esteem:
A belief in my potential; a
celebration of
my achievements; realizing
that the only
opinion that truly matters
is mine of me.

Laughter is
the perfect prayer.

Odds listen to
everyone's opinion
and take no one's advice.

Odds know that
the only things in life
that are in black and white
are the colors "black" and
"white."

The world is a sea of chaos,
each day bringing
a new wave of opportunities.

The customer is always
right—wrong! The customer
is always the customer.
Right and wrong have
nothing to do with it.

I'm perfect
and getting better.

The miserable ones—if you can't convert them, desert them, and move on.

If I can't get
past the gatekeeper,
I'll just jump
over the fence.

Odds never tie up their hands by holding grudges.

An odd knows an associate wants what's best for the associate; a friend wants what's best for both of you; and a lover wants what's best for you.

Sometimes to get
where I want to go
I have to begin
where I *don't* want to be.

Each of us is a rock
that sends ripples
through generations.

The world would be
a better place
if there were fewer
air conditioners
and more front porches.

I feed my mind
a healthy diet.

Life is learning.
Learning is life.
Always be getting better
at something.

You are not truly an adult
until you consider
all the children of the world
yours.

Everyday I listen
to the library.

Life is not fair.
So what?

School is school.
Life is life.

My odd is my ahead
not my behind.

Listen to
the fool.

I am the highlight
of everyone's day.

You do what's right
because it's right.
(The Jimmy Flasken Rule)

All odds are artists.
All artists are odd.

Who am I performing for?

Labels are for bottles,
cartons, and cans,
not people.

Am I hiding
or am I seeking?

Work is anything
I don't want to do.

If I haven't
committed a crime,
then I shouldn't be in jail.

There is a first time
and a last time
for everything.